L. Donald McVinney, MSSW
Editor

Chemical Dependency Treatment: Innovative Group Approaches

Chemical Dependency Treatment: Innovative Group Approaches has been co-published simultaneously as *Journal of Chemical Dependency Treatment*, Volume 7, Numbers 1/2 1997.

Pre-publication
REVIEWS,
COMMENTARIES,
EVALUATIONS . . .

"**C**hemical Dependency Treatment: *Innovative Group Approaches* is a comprehensive survey of innovative group approaches with addicted clients. It has practical examples of cognitive, behavioral, and psychotherapy groups in various treatment settings with clear guidelines for their implementation. Addtionally, it addresses the needs of clients with varying degrees of motivation for treatment. It includes strategies for motivational enhancement and for harm reduction. It is an excellent addition to the addiction treatment literature."

Barbara G. Faltz, RN, MS, CDNS
Inpatient Manager,
Addiction Treatment Services
Veterans Administration,
Palo Alto Health Care System

The Haworth Press, Inc.

Chemical Dependency Treatment: Innovative Group Approaches

Chemical Dependency Treatment: Innovative Group Approaches has been co-published simultaneously as *Journal of Chemical Dependency Treatment*, Volume 7, Numbers 1/2 1997.

The *Journal of Chemical Dependency Treatment* Monographs/ "Separates"

Chemical Dependency and Intimacy Dysfunction, edited by Eli Coleman

The Family Context of Adolescent Drug Use, edited by Robert H. Coombs

Practical Approaches in Treating Adolescent Chemical Dependency: A Guide to Clinical Assessment and Intervention, edited by Paul B. Henry

RELAPSE: Conceptual Research and Clinical Perspectives, edited by Dennis C. Daley

Aggression, Family Violence and Chemical Dependency, edited by Ronald T. Potter-Efron and Patricia S. Potter-Efron

Managing the Dually Diagnosed Patient: Current Issues and Clinical Approaches, edited by David F. O'Connell

Chemical Dependency: Theoretical Approaches and Strategies Working With Individuals and Families, edited by Eileen B. Isaacson

Counseling Chemically Dependent People With HIV Illness, edited by Michael Shernoff

Lesbians and Gay Men: Chemical Dependency Treatment Issues, edited by Dava L. Weinstein

Spirituality and Chemical Dependency, edited by Robert J. Kus

Chemical Dependency: Women at Risk, edited by Brenda L. Underhill

Chemical Dependency Treatment: Innovative Group Approaches, edited by L. Donald McVinney

These books were published simultaneously as special thematic issues of the *Journal of Chemical Dependency Treatment* and are available bound separately. Visit Haworth's website at http://www.haworth.com to search our online catalog for complete tables of contents and ordering information for these and other publications. Or call 1-800-HAWORTH (outside US/Canada: 607-722-5857), Fax: 1-800-895-0582 (outside US/Canada: 607-771-0012), or e-mail getinfo@haworth.com

Chemical Dependency Treatment: Innovative Group Approaches

L. Donald McVinney, MSSW
Editor

Chemical Dependency Treatment: Innovative Group Approaches has been co-published simultaneously as *Journal of Chemical Dependency Treatment*, Volume 7, Numbers 1/2 1997.

The Haworth Press, Inc.
New York • London

Chemical Dependency Treatment: Innovative Group Approaches has been co-published simultaneously as *Journal of Chemical Dependency Treatment*, Volume 7, Numbers 1/2 1997.

The development, preparation, and publication of this work has been undertaken with great care. However, the publisher, employees, editors, and agents of The Haworth Press and all imprints of The Haworth Press, Inc., including The Haworth Medical Press and Pharmaceutical Products Press, are not responsible for any errors contained herein or for consequences that may ensue from use of materials or information contained in this work. Opinions expressed by the author(s) are not necessarily those of The Haworth Press, Inc.

Cover design by Thomas J. Mayshock Jr.

The Haworth Press, Inc., 10 Alice Street, Binghamton, NY 13904-1580 USA

Library of Congress Cataloging-in-Publication Data

Chemical dependency treatment : innovative group approaches / L. Donald McVinney, editor.
     p. cm.
     "Has also been published as Journal of chemical dependency treatment, Volume 7, Numbers 1/2, 1997"–T.p. verso.
     Includes bibliographical references and index.
     ISBN 0-7890-0354-6 (alk. paper)
     1. Substance abuse–Treatment. 2. Group psychotherapy I. McVinney, L. Donald.
RC564.C4775 1997
616.86'0651–dc21
                                                 97-37554
                                                  CIP

INDEXING & ABSTRACTING

Contributions to this publication are selectively indexed or abstracted in print, electronic, online, or CD-ROM version(s) of the reference tools and information services listed below. This list is current as of the copyright date of this publication. See the end of this section for additional notes.

- **Academic Abstracts/CD-ROM,** EBSCO Publishing Editorial Department, P.O. Box 590, Ipswich, MA 01938-0690

- **ALCONLINE Database,** Centralforbundet for Alkohol-och narkotikaupplysning, Box 70412, 107 25 Stockholm, Sweden

- **Brown University Digest of Addiction Theory and Application, The (DATA Newsletter),** Project Cork Institute, Dartmouth Medical School, 14 S. Main Street, Suite 2F, Hanover, NH 03755-2015

- **Cambridge Scientific Abstracts,** 7200 Wisconsin Avenue #601, Bethesda, MD 20814

- **CNPIEC Reference Guide: Chinese National Directory of Foreign Periodicals,** P.O. Box 88, Beijing, Peoples Republic of China

- **Criminal Justice Abstracts,** Willow Tree Press, 15 Washington Street, 4th Floor, Newark, NJ 07102

- **Family Studies Database (online and CD-ROM),** National Information Services Corporation, 306 East Baltimore Pike, 2nd Floor, Media, PA 19063

- **Health Source: Indexing & Abstracting of 160 selected health related journals, updated monthly,** EBSCO Publishing, 83 Pine Street, Peabody, MA 01960

- **Health Source Plus: expanded version of "Health Source" to be released shortly,** EBSCO Publishing, 83 Pine Street, Peabody, MA 01960

(continued)

- *Index to Periodical Articles Related to Law,* University of Texas, 727 East 26th Street, Austin, TX 78705

- *INTERNET ACCESS (& additional networks) Bulletin Board for Libraries ("BUBL"), coverage of information resources on INTERNET, JANET, and other networks.*
  - <URL:http://bubl.ac.uk/>
  - The new locations will be found under <URL:http://bubl.ac. uk/link/>.
  - Any existing BUBL users who have problems finding information on the new service should contact the BUBL help line by sending e-mail to <bubl@bubl.ac.uk>.
  The Andersonian Library, Curran Building, 101 St. James Road, Glasgow G4 0NS, Scotland

- *Medication Use STudies (MUST) DATABASE,* The University of Mississippi, School of Pharmacy, University, MS 38677

- *Mental Health Abstracts (online through DIALOG),* IFI/Plenum Data Company, 3202 Kirkwood Highway, Wilmington, DE 19808

- *NIAAA Alcohol and Alcohol Problems Science Database (ETOH),* National Institute on Alcohol Abuse and Alcoholism, 1400 Eye Street NW, Suite 600, Washington, DC 20005

- *Referativnyi Zhurnal (Abstracts Journal of the Institute of Scientific Information of the Republic of Russia),* The Institute of Scientific Information, Baltijskaja ul., 14, Moscow A-219, Republic of Russia

- *Social Work Abstracts,* National Association of Social Workers, 750 First Street NW, 8th Floor, Washington, DC 20002

- *Sociological Abstracts (SA),* P.O. Box 22206, San Diego, CA 92192-0206

- *Special Educational Needs Abstracts,* Carfax Information Systems, P.O. Box 25, Abingdon, Oxfordshire OX14 3UE, United Kingdom

- *Violence and Abuse Abstracts: A Review of Current Literature on Interpersonal Violence (VAA),* Sage Publications, Inc., 2455 Teller Road, Newbury Park, CA 91320

SPECIAL BIBLIOGRAPHIC NOTES

related to special journal issues (separates)
and indexing/abstracting

☐ indexing/abstracting services in this list will also cover material in any "separate" that is co-published simultaneously with Haworth's special thematic journal issue or DocuSerial. Indexing/abstracting usually covers material at the article/chapter level.

☐ monographic co-editions are intended for either non-subscribers or libraries which intend to purchase a second copy for their circulating collections.

☐ monographic co-editions are reported to all jobbers/wholesalers/approval plans. The source journal is listed as the "series" to assist the prevention of duplicate purchasing in the same manner utilized for books-in-series.

☐ to facilitate user/access services all indexing/abstracting services are encouraged to utilize the co-indexing entry note indicated at the bottom of the first page of each article/chapter/contribution.

☐ this is intended to assist a library user of any reference tool (whether print, electronic, online, or CD-ROM) to locate the monographic version if the library has purchased this version but not a subscription to the source journal.

☐ individual articles/chapters in any Haworth publication are also available through the Haworth Document Delivery Service (HDDS).

Chemical Dependency Treatment: Innovative Group Approaches

CONTENTS

ABOUT THE EDITOR

L. Donald McVinney, MSSW, is Director of Triangle Treatment at the Robinson Institute, a New York State licensed outpatient chemical dependency program. He has worked in the addictions field for fifteen years as an administrator, direct service provider, program developer, trainer and educator. His primary interests are in the areas of substance use, gay and lesbian health issues, HIV/AIDS, and mental illness.

Introduction

This collection of essays has been conceptualized as a way to examine and present innovative group models of intervention with substance using and chemically dependent clients across the continuum of care. It is this editor's experience that although group work has traditionally been considered the primary modality in the treatment of chemically dependent clients (Anderson, 1983; Blume, 1985; Brown & Yalom, 1977; Flores, 1988; Khantzian, Halliday, & McAuliffe, 1990; Levine and Gallogly, 1985; Nace, 1987; Pita, 1994; Rogers & McMillan, 1984; Vanicelli, 1992), there is little information available for practitioners that are interested in exploring effective group intervention models at different stages of the treatment continuum, with clients at different stages of change regarding their chemical use, or with clients who present with unique needs.

Although this collection of essays begins to build upon the literature on the subject of group work within the chemical dependency field, it cannot be considered as inclusive. Nevertheless, this excellent collection of essays by experienced clinicians will be of considerable value to all practitioners in the field of chemical dependency.

This volume begins with a significant contribution to the literature by Eleanor C. Nealy that addresses an early group intervention model with active alcohol and other drug-using clients in a community-based setting. This model has been developed to address a service delivery gap in the substance abuse field that traditionally required individuals to first identify as addicts or alcoholics and

[Haworth co-indexing entry note]: "Introduction." McVinney, L. Donald. Co-published simultaneously in *Journal of Chemical Dependency Treatment* (The Haworth Press, Inc.) Vol. 7, No. 1/2, 1997, pp. 1-3; and: *Chemical Dependency Treatment: Innovative Group Approaches* (ed: L. Donald McVinney) The Haworth Press, Inc., 1997, pp. 1-3. Single or multiple copies of this article are available for a fee from The Haworth Document Delivery Service [1-800-342-9678, 9:00 a.m. - 5:00 p.m. (EST). E-mail address: getinfo@haworth.com].

1

then make a commitment to abstinence in order to begin, and remain, in treatment. As Nealy notes, "This approach is no longer acceptable, especially in the face of the ongoing AIDS epidemic." Her article describes an innovative group model designed to be implemented in a community-based agency setting.

Joseph H. Neisen provides an inpatient psychoeducational group model that has been developed for treating gay men and lesbians with alcohol and other drug abuse problems and describes the unique issues facing gay men and lesbians that need to be addressed by group services providers. Meredith Hanson's article then addresses the need to assist clients in connecting to outpatient clinics once they complete inpatient treatment. He presents an innovative transition group model developed for inner-city residents receiving inpatient alcoholism rehabilitation in a hospital-based alcoholism facility.

Curtis J. Brown presents a hospital-based early recovery group program for HIV-infected inner-city clients and discusses innovative strategies to engage clients in the program. His article also emphasizes the importance of effective ongoing needs assessment in order to understand the needs of clients and to provide successful group treatment. Shulamith Lala Ashenberg Straussner discusses the dynamics of substance-abusing clients and describes a model of treatment that is effective during the early phases of outpatient group therapy.

Fred Millán and Noel Elia present their innovative model of multiple oppression used in group psychotherapy with HIV-infected injecting drug users. The authors outline the various oppressed group memberships which impact on the lives of Black and Latino HIV-infected injecting drug users and describe effective group interventions.

In the article I co-authored with Darrell C. Greene, a group model is presented which focuses on a population of clients that are considered to be highly challenging to group facilitators, namely adult male clients who are chemically dependent and who have diagnosed personality disorders that are receiving services in an outpatient setting. This model combines interpersonal approaches with cognitive-behavioral intervention strategies.

Finally, I would like to express my sincere gratitude and appreciation to Dana Finnegan, PhD, CAC, Editor of the *Journal of Chemical Dependency Treatment,* for her support, encouragement, and patience in bringing this project to its successful conclusion.

L. Donald McVinney, MSSW, ACSW, CSW, CAC

REFERENCES

Anderson, S. C. (1983). Group therapy with alcoholic clients: A review. *Advances in Alcohol and Substance Abuse, 2*(2), 23-40.

Blume, S. B. (1985). Group psychotherapy in the treatment of alcoholism. In S. Zimberg, J. Wallace, & S.B. Blume (Eds.), pp.73-86. *Practical approaches to alcoholism psychotherapy* (2nd ed.). New York and London: Plenum Press.

Brown, S. & Yalom, I. (1977). Interactional group therapy with alcoholic patients. *Journal of Studies on Alcohol, 38,* 426-456.

Flores, P. J. (1988). *Group psychotherapy with addicted populations.* New York and London: The Haworth Press, Inc.

Khantzian, Halliday, & McAuliffe (1990). *Addiction and the vulnerable self: Modified dynamic group therapy for substance abusers.* New York: Guilford.

Levine, B. & Gallogly, V. (1985). *Group therapy with alcoholics: Outpatient and inpatient approaches.* Newbury Park, CA: Sage Publications.

Nace, E. P. (1987). *The treatment of alcoholism.* New York: Brunner/Mazel.

Pita, D. D. (1994). *Addictions counseling. A practical guide to counseling people with chemical and other addictions.* New York: Crossroad.

Rogers, R. & McMillan, C. (1984). *Don't help. A guide to working with the alcoholic.* West Friendship, Maryland: Education and Training Institute of Maryland.

Vanicelli, M. (1992). *Removing the roadblocks: Group psychotherapy with substance abusers and family members.* New York: Guilford.

Early Intervention with Active Drug and Alcohol Users in Community-Based Settings

Eleanor C. Nealy, MDiv, MSSW, CSW

SUMMARY. In light of recent knowledge regarding the nature of addiction, as well as the pressing impetus of the AIDS epidemic, clinicians must seek out new approaches that enable earlier intervention. This article describes one such model designed for implementation in a community-based agency setting. *[Article copies available for a fee from The Haworth Document Delivery Service: 1-800-342-9678. E-mail address: getinfo@haworth.com]*

INTRODUCTION

The relationship between injection drug use (IDU) and HIV transmission has been well established. Injecting drug use continues to be the second most common risk behavior associated with AIDS in the United States (CDC, 1993). Numerous studies document sharing of needles and other drug injection paraphernalia among IDUs as a major mode of HIV transmission (Battjes, 1994).

In addition, increasing concerns have emerged about the contribution of non-IDUs to HIV transmission and disease progression.

Address correspondence to: Eleanor Nealy, MDiv, MSSW, CSW, 7601 Greenlee, Fort Worth, TX 76112.

[Haworth co-indexing entry note]: "Early Intervention with Active Drug and Alcohol Users in Community-Based Settings." Nealy, Eleanor C. Co-published simultaneously in *Journal of Chemical Dependency Treatment* (The Haworth Press, Inc.) Vol. 7, No. 1/2, 1997, pp. 5-20; and: *Chemical Dependency Treatment: Innovative Group Approaches* (ed: L. Donald McVinney) The Haworth Press, Inc., 1997, pp. 5-20. Single or multiple copies of this article are available for a fee from The Haworth Document Delivery Service [1-800-342-9678, 9:00 a.m. - 5:00 p.m. (EST). E-mail address: getinfo@haworth.com].

Recent studies have suggested that crack cocaine users who engage in sex to obtain their drugs may be at especially high risk for HIV infection (Inciardi et al., 1993; Ratner, 1993). Other concerns include the ways in which drug and alcohol use may lessen inhibition and facilitate engagement in sexual risk behaviors. Several studies have found a strong relationship between the use of drugs and/or alcohol and noncompliance with safe sex techniques (Allen, 1994; Leigh, 1990; Stall, 1988). In a study of Massachusetts teenagers, Hingson et al. (1990) similarly concluded that drug and alcohol use was consistently associated with unsafe sexual practices.

These reports have led to a call to alter the nature of HIV education and prevention work. For example, as Stall (1988, p. 80) concludes, "whatever the cause behind this association, the strength of the association between combining sexual activity with drug and/or alcohol use and high risk sexual behavior is so strong and the consequences of HIV infection so profound that health education campaigns to communicate the fact of this association to populations at high risk of HIV infection seem justified."

However, the substance abuse field has been slow to respond to these concerns. Traditional treatment models generally require individuals to identify as addicts or alcoholics and make a commitment to abstinence in order to begin, and remain in, treatment. Individuals who refuse to commit to abstinence, or who repeatedly relapse, are viewed as being "in denial" and are told to "come back when you're ready." This approach is no longer acceptable, especially in the face of the ongoing AIDS epidemic. Given the overwhelming evidence regarding the association between alcohol and drug use and unsafe sexual behavior, treatment providers can no longer wait for users to become self-motivated before beginning intervention.

In reality, refusing to engage substance users until it is easier and more convenient for us as clinicians, i.e., when they are ready to commit to abstinence, has probably never been tenable from an ethical or clinical perspective. In light of recent knowledge regarding the nature of addiction, as well as the pressing impetus of the AIDS epidemic, clinicians must seek out new approaches that enable earlier intervention. This article describes one such model designed for implementation in a community-based agency setting.

THEORETICAL FRAMEWORK

This model is based on research by James Prochaska and Carlo DiClemente (1982) which identified five stages of changing addictive behaviors. While the original research was rooted in nicotine addiction, the model has since been applied to a wide range of behavior changes including varying drug and alcohol use, diet and weight control, exercise adoption, and safer sex behaviors (Prochaska et al., 1994).

In the first stage, *Pre-Contemplation,* individuals perceive no problem with their drug and alcohol use and thus see no reason to change their use patterns, nor any reason to develop motivation toward change. While friends, family or employers may identify drug or alcohol-related problems, the individual's primary experience of his/her substance use is positive. Consequently, individuals in pre-contemplation rarely present for drug and alcohol treatment unless they are pressured or mandated to do so by external forces.

During the second stage, *Contemplation,* individuals have begun to experience some negative consequences associated with their drug and alcohol use and thus are more open to information and feedback from others. Contemplators have a beginning awareness of their need to make changes but are characterized by a reluctance to take action. While they have begun to identify the negative consequences of their use patterns, they still attribute many positive experiences to their use. In addition, they are anxious about change and possess many doubts about their ability to effect changes. These dynamics keep them mired in ambivalence and prevent action towards change. Miller (1989, p. 70) has described the contemplation stage as an "internal seesaw which rocks back and forth between motivation to change on the one side and to stay the same on the other." Individuals may remain in the contemplation stage for long periods of time.

Stage three, *Preparation* (also called "Determination" or "Pre-action"), combines intention and action. In essence, this stage reflects an internal movement forward that results in a decisive mental commitment to change. People move from contemplation to preparation when the positive benefits of change outweigh the negative costs of change. In this stage, individuals begin to envision change, to believe that change will benefit them, and to trust that they are capable of effecting this change. They often begin taking small steps that will lead to their overall change objective.

Stage four, *Action,* reflects the point at which most individuals become engaged with traditional drug and alcohol treatment. In this stage, they make a decision to follow through on a plan of action developed during the previous stage and become actively involved in modifying their behavior, experiences, or environment in order to overcome their problem(s). In traditional addiction treatment, this represents the point at which an individual becomes abstinent and embarks on a program of recovery.

Stage five, *Maintenance,* represents a continuation of, not an absence of, change. The major focus is relapse prevention. Key tasks include consolidating the gains made during the action stage and dealing with the struggles created by the changes one has made, i.e., lifestyle changes, experiencing new emotions, and social, familial, or intimate relationship changes.

Several points about this model must be noted. First, Prochaska and DiClemente present this model as a spiral, a paradigm whose primary point is to convey a continuum of change (Prochaska et al., 1992). As they note, "people, including professionals, often erroneously equate action with change, [thus overlooking] the requisite work that prepares changers for action and the important efforts necessary to maintain the changes following action" (p. 1104).

Second, while linear progression is possible, it is not the norm. Most people cycle back and forth, moving in and out of different stages. Furthermore, individuals may be in more than one stage at a time. For example, a client may be in action in terms of their alcohol use, but in pre-contemplation regarding their marijuana use.

Third, research studies consistently document the fact that most individuals cycle through the stages numerous times before gaining the skills and experience necessary for successful maintenance (Schacter, 1982; Norcross & Vangarelli, 1989). With this understanding, relapse becomes not only an important, but perhaps even an essential, component of the learning process. Relapsers may immediately re-engage in the action stage or they may return to an earlier stage. However, research does suggest that most relapsers do not revolve endlessly in circles, nor do they regress all the way back to where they began (Prochaska et al., 1992). Recognizing relapse as a normal phase in the continuum of change can be a useful teaching tool about change for active drug and alcohol users, as well as a helpful antidote to despair about failure when relapse does occur.

In reflecting on this staged approach, it is clear that traditional drug and alcohol treatment, with its requirement for abstinence, has been designed for individuals who are at least in the preparation, and preferably, the action stage. However, the vast majority of addicted individuals are not in the action stage. As identified in the introduction, this approach of refraining from clinical intervention until clients are "motivated" is no longer acceptable. Motivation for change must be actively promoted, rather than passively awaited.

PROGRAM DEVELOPMENT

The model described in this article reflects a joint program developed over the past few years as a collaborative project of two New York City community-based agencies: the Gay Men's Health Crisis (GMHC) and Project Connect of the Lesbian and Gay Community Services Center. As a multifaceted social service agency with a commitment to serving the needs of individuals living with HIV/AIDS, GMHC had historically had few substance abuse-related services. Project Connect, established in 1988, is a New York State Office of Alcoholism and Substance Abuse Services (OASAS)-certified alcohol and other drug prevention and intervention program. As a part of the Lesbian and Gay Community Services Center's Mental Health and Social Service Department, Project Connect seeks to deliver client services within the framework of community-building and lesbian, gay, bisexual and transgender liberation and empowerment.

Initially, Project Connect began working with GMHC to offer recovery support groups on-site at GMHC to individuals living with AIDS. In the course of facilitating these groups, it became apparent that there were numerous persons struggling with issues of chronic relapse, for whom traditional treatment had been unsuccessful. There were also other individuals who had concerns about the ways their drug and/or alcohol use, or the combination of their substance use and their sexual behavior, was affecting their health but did not identify as addicts or alcoholics and simply were not ready to commit to abstinence. As a result, the early recovery groups failed to effectively meet their needs. Still, it seemed that their ability and willingness to articulate their concerns warranted some response by the agencies involved.

The initial model utilized by Project Connect and GMHC was group-based with the primary service being a ten week group designed to enable participants to assess their relationship to drugs and alcohol and sexual behaviors, and to begin identifying and effecting behavioral changes. The additional components included biweekly individual counseling focused on enhancing motivation and goal-setting, and ear point acupuncture.

This model has since evolved into two separate programs: Project Connect expanded its traditional recovery interventions to include more recovery-readiness work, and GMHC created a new department, Substance Use and Counseling Education (SUCE), whose primary mission is recovery-readiness counseling. The ideas reflected in this article are the result of collaborative work between Project Connect staff and Richard Elovich, Director of SUCE, and other SUCE staff.

The model developed by Prochaska and DiClemente contributed to the theoretical framework for the recovery-readiness program that emerged. Recovery-readiness represents an expansion of the harm reduction model (developed in the context of HIV/AIDS prevention and education) whose primary principles can be summarized as follows:

1. Abstinence should not be the only objective of services to drug users because it excludes a large proportion of the people who are committed to long term drug use.
2. Abstinence should be conceptualized as the final goal in a series of harm-reduction objectives, objectives which seek to reduce the harm that drug use causes.
3. The most effective way of getting people to minimize the harmful effects of their drug use is to provide user-friendly services which attract them into contact and empower them to change their behavior toward a suitable intermediate objective (Springer, 1995).

For a more thorough discussion of the harm reduction model in conjunction with addiction treatment, see Elovich and Cowing (1995) and Marlatt and Tapert (1993).

The Prochaska-DiClemente model takes a proactive role in building motivation for change. By avoiding the demand that participants be committed to abstinence, or to any particular change goal, it allows clinicians to work with individuals wherever they may fall along the spectrum of substance use. The model is client-centered, rather than clinician- or agency-centered. Thus, counselors work cooperatively with individuals to empower them to set their own priorities for change and develop their own timeline for action, rather than assuming a hierarchy of issues to be addressed. Furthermore, in tailoring clinical work to match where each person is along the continuum of change, the effectiveness of clinician intervention is significantly increased and worker frustration with client progress is decreased (Elovich & Oliveira, 1995a).

Utilizing a group work model is critical to the implementation of this program. First, the group offers an opportunity to experience oneself in the presence of others, thus breaking down the isolation, fear and shame which surrounds so many of the participants. Second, the group represents a mirroring process where individuals can observe or experience similarities or contrasts in thoughts, feelings, beliefs, and actions. In doing so, the group becomes an opportunity to witness and model a peer transformational process. In essence, each member becomes a "peer educator"; each member's successes and failures become teaching tools. In the course of group interactions, members become aware of their ability to have an impact on their peers, thereby enhancing self-esteem and self-efficacy. Third, the group experience provides clear parameters or limits for interaction and growth. Over time, the group becomes a "container" for the individual process of change. Fourth, the group provides immediate and ongoing support for the development of alternative social networks that reinforce the process of change (Elovich & Oliveira, 1995b).

One criticism of the Prochaska-DiClemente model involves the extent to which its cognitive-behavioral framework may fail to address the emotional and/or environmental dynamics which impact an individual's ability to successfully effect change. As Barber

(1994, p. 44) notes, Prochaska and DiClemente "fail to grasp the inescapably social context within which all individuals live and move and have their being." In addressing the external forces which may inhibit change, it is essential to examine the substance user's interpersonal relationships, as well as the systems, structures, and larger forces which often debilitate self-esteem and self-competence, and consequently preclude change and growth.

In an effort to address these issues, the curriculum developed for the Project Connect/GMHC program was designed to function on three levels. The first, cognitive, includes aspects such as teaching the Prochaska-DiClemente approach, addressing costs and benefits of drug and alcohol use, and increasing awareness regarding current use patterns.

The second level, emotional, involves contextualizing the Prochaska-DiClemente model. As human beings, no one makes changes in a vacuum. The state of our self-esteem and self-confidence, the strengths and weaknesses of our interpersonal relationships, the extent of our social support networks, the stability of basic survival needs such as housing, sufficient income, and decent and accessible medical care, all affect our ability to make change successfully.

The third level, relational, continues the contextualization of the change model. In contrast to traditional therapy groups which tend to limit member interaction outside of the group session, Project Connect/GMHC groups place a premium on developing a peer support network both within and outside of group. Recognizing that support is essential to successful behavioral change, members are encouraged to exchange phone numbers and are given homework assignments to call and check in with others between the group sessions. There is a clear, overt focus on the development of intimacy and support within the group. The ways in which members learn to connect with one another in the session is viewed as skills-building and is held up as a reflection of what they are capable of beginning to do outside the group.

Group Purpose

The primary group purpose is two-fold: early intervention for drug and alcohol use/misuse, and HIV prevention, both the prevention of seroconversion as well as prevention of disease progression in persons living with HIV/AIDS.

Advertising for these groups is targeted at individuals who have concerns about the ways their use of drugs or alcohol and/or their sexual behavior may be affecting their health. In other words, they are designed to attract persons in the contemplation stage, people who have concerns about their use, but are not ready for abstinence. The ads are non-clinical in their language and are explicit in stating that one need not identify as an addict or an alcoholic in order to seek help (see Miller & Rollnick (1991), pp. 58-59, regarding the acceptance of labels as unnecessary).

Given their target audience, these groups do not require a commitment to abstinence. "Showing up," or attending group each week, is emphasized as the primary commitment, along with the willingness to participate as honestly as possible. The issue of whether it is acceptable to show up for group while high or intoxicated is addressed in the first group. Rather than create rules which might invite client resistance, members are encouraged to explore this issue from the perspective of our human need to "take a few steps back" from something in order to accurately assess our relationship to it. While behavior that is disruptive to the group is not tolerated, participants attending group high or drunk has been minimal.

Group Composition

All groups require a pre-group screening interview, ideally with a clinician who will be one of the group's facilitators (most of the groups have been co-facilitated). During this session, it is essential to complete a thorough assessment regarding where the individual is along the Prochaska-DiClemente continuum. When possible, we have found it useful to work with clients individually for two or three sessions before placing them in a group. These sessions focus on helping the client gain increased clarity regarding their concerns about their drug and alcohol use and addressing their fears and ambivalence regarding group participation. Both have resulted in clients being more fully prepared for the group experience and thus able to participate more effectively. To a large extent, these sessions incorporate Miller and Rollnick's (1991) work on motivational counseling.

Agency early recovery support groups, comprised of persons committed to sobriety and thus in the action or maintenance stages, had typically been able to tolerate a wide range of differences. Similarly, the first groups in the recovery-readiness program were extremely heterogenous, open to anyone with concerns about their drug and alcohol use. Membership included men and women across a wide range of ages, racial/ethnic backgrounds, and sexual orientations. However, group dynamics and retention in the new program were more problematic.

Over time it became apparent that since these groups were comprised of persons in the contemplation stage for which ambivalence is the hallmark, too much difference only added to members' difficulties in engaging. While always a significant group consideration, homogeneity seemed even more critical if this population was to bond and successfully become a group. Consequently, groups were developed with a more homogenous membership and focus. This also allowed for a more specific development of the contextualization of the change process. Examples of these groups include: gay men who are HIV+ and/or living with AIDS, gay men whose status is HIV- or untested, young gay men ages 18-25 years, lesbians, and young lesbians ages 18-25 years old.

Group Content

The groups begin with a focus on ambivalence, the hallmark of the contemplation stage. Each member has an opportunity to identify and share their presenting concerns about the ways their drug and alcohol use or sexual behavior may be affecting their health or lives. In fact, during the first session, attention is paid to eliciting and addressing members' ambivalence about participating in the group itself, identifying their fears and anxieties, as well as their expectations and hopes about joining the group.

During the first and second groups, facilitators focus on drawing out members' ambivalence with two-sided questions that reflect the contextualization of the change process. For example: How does using drugs or alcohol make it easier to live with HIV and AIDS? What concerns do you have about the ways your drug or alcohol use may be affecting your health or HIV status? How does using drugs and alcohol make it easier to live as a gay man in New York City? What concerns do you have about the ways drugs and alcohol are affecting your life? How does using drugs and alcohol make it easier to navigate family, social, or intimate relationships? What concerns do you have about the ways drugs and alcohol are affecting your relationships?

It is particularly important to focus on drawing out each client's perception of the positive benefits of their substance use. It is precisely these positive perceptions and experiences that keep individuals in the contemplation stage. As Barber (1994, p. 95) notes, people utilize drugs and alcohol in order to cope more effectively with their varying life experiences, and successful treatment lies in "delineating the positive consequences of . . . abuse and finding ways of substituting more adaptive behaviors to achieve these ends."

Unfortunately many clinicians, especially those trained in traditional substance abuse treatment, have a tendency to gloss over these positive perceptions in a rush to confront denial and highlight the negative consequences. However, unless a client's ambivalence is fully engaged, and both the positive and negative consequences of use explored, the individual will be unable to effectively make and/or maintain behavioral change (Barber, 1994). It should also be noted here that the Prochaska-DiClemente framework redefines "denial" as "ambivalence," a concept that is infinitely less pejorative and blaming, and thus more likely to empower change (Miller, 1989).

In keeping with Miller and Rollnick's (1991) emphasis on affirmation as a key aspect of building client motivation, group facilitators provide overt and ongoing affirmation of members, especially during initial sessions, for example, validating the courage it takes to show up for the first group, affirming members' willingness to talk about "tough issues," acknowledging the facilitator's respect for participants' life struggles and accomplishments. Early on in the group cycle, participants are taught the Prochaska-DiClemente staged model for changing behaviors. They are encouraged to utilize this framework to reflect on their own needs and assess their place along the continuum of change in regard to joining the group, their drug and/or alcohol use, and their safer sex behavior patterns.

Generally the third session focuses in a very specific way on group building and connecting. For example, in gay and lesbian groups a meditation exercise that elicits coming out stories is often utilized. In groups for people living with HIV and AIDS, a similar exercise has been created that encourages members to tell their stories of when they first suspected they were HIV-positive, when they actually found out, who they told first, etc. This kind of story-telling generates profound emotional bonding which sets the stage for the remainder of the group sessions.

In the middle section, much focus is placed on gaining increased awareness regarding one's patterns of drug and alcohol use. Daily use logs are assigned as homework, in which members are asked to write down each time they use in as much detail as possible, including such factors as how much they used, where they were, who they were with, what they were feeling, etc.

Participants are taught the Antecedent-Behavior-Consequence paradigm (Ellis, 1975) and encouraged to utilize this framework in their logs. These worksheets are processed in both group and individual sessions and serve several functions. First, they provide concrete information which helps clients become clear about how much and how frequently they actually engage in drug and alcohol use. Second, they provide rich information about the feeling states that tend to trigger the desire to get high. Third, they serve to increase cognitive dissonance. As Miller and Rollnick (1991) define it, this means highlighting the discrepancies between present behavior and broader goals, between where one is and where one wants to be. During both group and individual sessions, clinicians take an active role in helping clients clarify personal values and goals and explore how their present drug or alcohol use facilitates or precludes attaining these goals. Clients are encouraged to identify what they were looking for when they got high, and then to explore whether or not getting high or drunk enabled them to obtain what they wanted. For example, if they set out for the bar because they were "lonely and wanted to connect," did they end up feeling less lonely after they got high? How did they feel the next morning? Many times this work creates an opening to begin discussing whether there might be more effective ways to get their needs met.

Later groups focus on teaching the skills necessary to effect change, particularly goal-setting that is concrete, specific, and attainable. Members learn to identify common barriers to change, including the use of defense mechanisms. Members set goals for themselves in the group and report back on their progress in the following groups. They are taught to coach one another to be specific, to think through possible obstacles and how they will respond to them if they occur. Each goal successfully achieved builds self-efficacy, "a person's belief in his or her ability to carry out and succeed with a specific task" (Miller & Rollnick, 1991). The belief in one's ability to effect change is well documented as a key aspect of motivation for change (Bandura, 1982; Goldman & Harlow, 1993; Kelly et al., 1990) and a critical factor in one's ability to maintain change (DiClemente et al., 1985; Solomon and Annis, 1990; Wilkinson and LeBreton, 1986).

In the course of facilitating group process, emphasis is placed on building emotional skills, enhancing members' ability to identify, tolerate, and constructively express their feelings. Particular attention is paid to identifying and developing alternative coping mechanisms and building healthy support networks that nurture the changes they attempt to effect. The group becomes a laboratory for this process, with contact outside of the group encouraged.

In regard to contextualizing the model, the group's membership generally suggests the content. In groups for people who are HIV+, the stressors and challenges of living with HIV/AIDS become a major focus. In groups for lesbians and gay men, much time is spent processing issues of coming out, moving beyond internalized homophobia and shame, and developing a proud gay identity. Gender socialization, and the ways it affects our ability to express emotions and build intimate relationships, as well as broader conversations regarding intimacy and self-disclosure, have been important themes in all of the groups. In the 18-25 year old groups, developmental issues surrounding leaving home, establishing an adult self-image, and finding a place within the adult community have formed the core of important discussions. In all of these themes, the facilitator's role is to help members make the connections between these issues and their use of drugs or alcohol, i.e., how have we used drugs and alcohol to alter our feelings, to help us feel connected to others, to ease our anxieties about intimacy, etc.

CONCLUSION

The program described in this article is not a finished project. It is continually evolving as staff and clients work together to enhance its effectiveness. While the early sessions of the group are fairly consistent in their focus, later sessions tend to incorporate the particular issues of that group, rather than follow a prescribed curriculum order.

Over time, it has become apparent that for many participants, especially those in pre-contemplation or in the early part of the contemplation stage, a ten week group is insufficient. While acknowledging the progress they had made in ten weeks, group members themselves insisted on more. Consequently, the SUCE/GMHC program has become a series of three, sequential ten week groups. In the adolescent/young adult groups operating at Project Connect, participants are allowed to "carry-over" from one ten week cycle into the next.

While this program was developed for use within two community-based organizations, its basic principles could easily be applied to a wide variety of health care or substance abuse treatment settings. Implementation in the former would allow for earlier assessment of and intervention with problem users. Providing recovery-readiness groups within outpatient chemical dependency treatment facilities would create a broader continuum of care, thus enabling better client-program fit for those persons presenting for treatment while still in the contemplation or preparation stages of change.

Working with individuals who are in the pre-contemplation or contemplation stages of change, responding to their ambivalence, working to enhance their motivation toward change, is a complex and challenging endeavor. It demands that clinicians explore new concepts regarding the nature of addiction, grapple with old biases regarding addicts and alcoholics, relinquish cherished notions of what recovery is and how it ought to happen. Given the ongoing devastation of untreated substance abuse and the HIV/AIDS epidemic, it is a challenge that must be addressed.

REFERENCES

Allen, K. (1994). Female drug abusers and the context of their HIV transmission risk behaviors. In Battjes, R.J., Sloboda, Z., & Grace, W.C. (Eds.), The context of HIV risk among drug users and their sexual partners. *National Institute on Drug Abuse (NIDA) Research Monograph 143.* Rockville, MD: NIDA.

Bandura, A. (1982). Self-efficacy mechanism in human agency. *American Psychologist, 37,* 122-147.

Barber, J.G. (1994). *Social work with addictions.* NY: New York University Press.

Battjes, R.J., Sloboda, Z., & Grace, W.C. (1994). The context of HIV risk among drug users and their sexual partners. *National Institute on Drug Abuse (NIDA) Research Monograph 143.* Rockville, MD: NIDA.

Centers for Disease Control and Prevention (1993). *HIV/AIDS Surveillance Report, 5(3).*

DiClemente, C.C., Prochaska, J.O., & Gilbertini, M. (1985). Self-efficacy and the stages of self-change in smoking. *Cognitive Therapy and Research, 9,* 181-200.

Ellis, A., & Harper, R.A. (1975). *A new guide to rational living.* Hollywood, CA: Wilshire Books.

Elovich, R.E., & Cowing, M. (1995). Recovery-readiness: Strategies that bring treatment to addicts where they are. In *Harm Reduction and Steps Toward Change: A Training Sourcebook.* New York: The Gay Men's Health Crisis.

Elovich, R.E., & Oliviera, A. (1995a). Steps toward change. In *LAP NOTES: Lesbian AIDS Project at GMHC, 3,* 8-9.

Elovich, R.E., & Oliviera, A. (1995b). Steps toward change: Working with ambivalence and building motivation for change. In *Harm Reduction and Steps Toward Change: A Training Sourcebook.* New York: The Gay Men's Health Crisis.

Goldman, J.A., & Harlow, L.L. (1993). Self-perception variables that mediate AIDS-preventive behavior in college students. *Health Psychologist, 12,* 489-493.

Hingson, R.W., Strunin, L., Berlin, B.M., & Heeren, T. (1990). Beliefs about AIDS, use of alcohol and drugs, and unprotected sex among Massachusetts adolescents. *American Journal of Public Health, 80(3),* 295-299.

Inciardi, J.A., Lockwood, D., & Pottieger, A.E. (1993) *Women and Crack-Cocaine.* New York: Macmillan.

Kelly, J.A., Lawrence, J.S., Brasfield, T.L., Lemke, A., Amidei, T., Roffman, R.E., Hood, H.V., Smith, J.E., Kilgore, H., & McNeill, C. (1990). Psychological factors that predict AIDS high-risk versus AIDS precautionary behavior. *Journal of Consulting and Clinical Psychology, 58,* 117-120.

Leigh, B.C. (1990). Relationship of substance use during sex to high-risk sexual behavior. *Journal of Sexual Research, 27(2),* 199-213.

Marlatt, G.A., & Tapert, S.F. (1993). Harm reduction: Reducing the risks of addictive behaviors. In J.S. Baer, G.A. Marlatt, & R.J. McMahon (Eds.), *Addictive Behaviors Across the Lifespan: Prevention, Treatment, and Policy Issues.* Newbury Park, CA: Sage Publications.

Miller, W.R. (1989). Increasing motivation for change. In R. Hester & W. Miller (Eds.), *Handbook of Alcoholism Treatment Approaches.* New York: Pergamon Press.

Miller, W.R., & Rollnick, S. (1991). *Motivational Interviewing: Preparing People to Change Addictive Behavior.* New York: Guilford Press.

Norcross, J.C., & Vangarelli, D.J. (1989). The resolution solution: Longitudinal examination of New Year's attempts. *Journal of Substance Abuse, 1,* 127-134.

Prochaska, J., & DiClemente, C. (1982). Transtheoretical therapy: Toward a more integrative model of change. *Psychotherapy: Theory, Research, and Practice, 19,* 276-288.

Prochaska, J., DiClemente, C., & Norcross, J. (1992). In search of how people change: Applications to addictive behaviors. *American Psychologist, 47(9),* 1101-1113.

Prochaska, J., Redding, C.A., Harlow, L.L., Rossi, J.S., & Velicer, W.F. (1994). The transtheoretical model of change and HIV prevention: A review. *Health Education Quarterly, 21(4),* 471-486.

Ratner, M.S., Ed. (1993). *Crack Pipe as Pimp: An Ethnographic Investigation of Sex-for-Crack Exchanges.* New York: Lexington Books.

Schachter, S. (1982). Recidivism and self-cure of smoking and obesity. *American Psychologist, 37,* 436-444.

Solomon, K.E., & Annis, H.M. (1990). Outcome and efficacy expectancy in the prediction of post-treatment drinking behavior. *British Journal of Addiction, 85,* 659-665.

Springer, E. (1995). Harm reduction model: For working with drug users during the AIDS epidemic. In *Harm Reduction and Steps Toward Change: A Training Sourcebook.* New York: The Gay Men's Health Crisis.

Stall, R. (1988). The prevention of HIV infection associated with alcohol and drug use during sexual activity. In L. Siegel (Ed.), *AIDS and Substance Abuse* (pp. 73-88). New York: Harrington Park Press.

Wilkinson, D.A., & LeBreton, S. (1986). Early indications of treatment outcome in multiple drug users. In W.R. Miller & N. Heather (Eds.), *Treating Addictive Behaviors: Processes of Change* (pp. 239-261). New York: Plenum Press.

The Transition Group: Linking Clients with Alcohol Problems to Outpatient Care

Meredith Hanson, DSW

SUMMARY. This article describes a transition group developed for inner city residents receiving inpatient alcoholism rehabilitation in a hospital-based alcoholism facility. The goal of the group was to facilitate clients' transition from inpatient to outpatient alcoholism treatment. First, the paper will suggest reasons why clients do not continue in care, and it will review prior efforts to help people connect with continuing outpatient treatment. Then, the theoretical framework that guided the group's design will be described. Next, it will outline the intervention's components. Finally, it will discuss the group's effectiveness and implications for clinical practice with adults who experience alcohol problems. *[Article copies available for a fee from The Haworth Document Delivery Service: 1-800-342-9678. E-mail address: getinfo@haworth.com]*

Programs for adults suffering from alcohol problems have long been organized into stages or phases that provide a continuum-of-

Meredith Hanson is Associate Professor, Fordham University Graduate School of Social Service. He has worked in the addictions field for over twenty-five years as a clinician, program developer, supervisor, administrator, researcher, and educator. His primary areas of interest involve working with clients with dual diagnoses, HIV/AIDS prevention with substance abusers, and motivational interviewing.

Address correspondence to: Dr. Meredith Hanson, Graduate School of Social Service, Fordham University, Lincoln Center Campus, 113 West 60th Street, New York, NY 10023.

[Haworth co-indexing entry note]: "The Transition Group: Linking Clients with Alcohol Problems to Outpatient Care." Hanson, Meredith. Co-published simultaneously in *Journal of Chemical Dependency Treatment* (The Haworth Press, Inc.) Vol. 7, No. 1/2, 1997, pp. 21-35; and: *Chemical Dependency Treatment: Innovative Group Approaches* (ed: L. Donald McVinney) The Haworth Press, Inc., 1997, pp. 21-35. Single or multiple copies of this article are available for a fee from The Haworth Document Delivery Service [1-800-342-9678, 9:00 a.m. - 5:00 p.m. (EST). E-mail address: getinfo@haworth.com].

care framework for treatment services (Glaser, Greenberg, & Barrett, 1978; Institute of Medicine, 1990; Pattison, 1985). This structure, which usually includes detoxification services, inpatient or residential rehabilitation, and some form of outpatient treatment, is designed to be responsive to the differential needs of clients who enter treatment at different points in recovery. Most clinicians believe that outpatient care is necessary for clients to avoid relapse and maintain sobriety. Their beliefs are supported by the research literature, which documents a positive association between continuance in treatment and beneficial therapeutic outcomes (Ito & Donovan, 1986; Stark, 1992). Spurred by health care reform and dissatisfaction with the effectiveness of treatment, emphasis has focused on improving the continuity and coordination of care and redirecting intervention efforts toward community-based and outpatient services (Moos & Finney, 1995).

Despite the prevailing beliefs, empirical evidence, and pressures from consumers and legislators, helping clients connect with outpatient clinics once they complete inpatient treatment remains one of the most difficult tasks in the alcoholism treatment field. Significant numbers of clients minimize the need for continuing care, encounter nonsupportive environments, and either refuse alcoholism outpatient services or drop out of treatment shortly after intake (Castaneda et al., 1992; Kirk & Masi, 1978; Pratt et al., 1977; Stark, 1992). Among the clients who are least likely to use outpatient services are members of society's most oppressed groups–impoverished persons, individuals who are socially alienated and isolated, and people experiencing comorbid psychopathology and substance use disorders (Fagan & Mauss, 1986; Verinis, 1995; Waisberg, 1990).

This article describes a transition group developed for inner city residents receiving inpatient alcoholism rehabilitation in a hospital-based alcoholism facility. The goal of the group was to facilitate clients' transition from inpatient to outpatient alcoholism treatment. First, the paper will suggest reasons why clients do not continue in care, and it will review prior efforts to help people connect with continuing outpatient treatment. Then, the theoretical framework that guided the group's design will be described. Next, it will outline the intervention's components. Finally, it will discuss the group's effectiveness and implications for clinical practice with adults who experience alcohol problems.

NATURE OF THE PROBLEM

Several client-related factors are associated with lower rates of contact with continuing outpatient treatment. As noted above, persons who are socially disadvantaged and possess fewer resources are less likely than others to continue in treatment (Verinis, 1995; Waisberg, 1990). Also, clients who feel less confident in their abilities to resist pressures to resume drinking have lower rates of follow through with continuing care than do persons who feel more self-efficacious (Hanson et al., under review). Third, individuals who are uncertain about the presence and severity of drinking-related problems tend not to initiate and follow through with self-change efforts (Prochaska, DiClemente, & Norcross, 1992). Finally, clients who are unaware of the resources that are available to help them maintain sobriety and those who have doubts about the usefulness of those resources are less likely to use treatment (Rosenstock, Strecher, & Becker, 1988).

Interventions designed to help clients enter outpatient alcoholism clinics have produced mixed results. Novick and his colleagues (1974) discovered, for example, that over one-third of a sample of inner city men who completed alcohol detoxification did not return to an alcoholism clinic despite being escorted to a first visit by an inpatient counselor. Verinis and Taylor (1994) reported that having a counselor who would continue to work with them in aftercare had no impact on aftercare follow through among men who completed inpatient alcohol rehabilitation. Likewise, Alterman and co-workers (1994) found that replacing a substance abuse day treatment program's waiting list with a three day per week orientation group did not lower attrition.

In contrast to the preceding findings, several investigators have reported on outpatient groups, which improved retention rates in alcoholism clinics (Dolan, 1975; Gallant, 1987; Levinson, 1979; Verinis & Taylor, 1994). These groups oriented new clients to clinic procedures, educated them about the adverse consequences of alcohol abuse, and provided supportive contexts within which to make decisions about continuing in treatment. Other researchers have found that, when these types of groups are initiated on inpatient units, their presence is associated with higher follow through rates with outpatient treatment. Panepinto and his colleagues (1980; Galanter & Panepinto, 1980) found that inpatients who attended group orientation sessions before entering outpatient treatment were more apt than persons who did not receive orientation sessions to return to an alcoholism outpatient clinic (71% vs. 53%). Verinis (1984) discovered that a discharge planning group, which encouraged inpatients to plan for aftercare, oriented them to outpatient treatment, and provided them with the names of resources, improved follow through rates from 14% to 19%. By modifying the inpatient rehabilitation program further so that more systematic attention was directed at continuing care by the entire staff, the follow through rate increased to 41%. Kofoed and Keys (1988) reported that group-based strategies that drew participants' attention to the negative impact of substance use and allowed them to learn from each others' experiences helped inpatients with comorbid substance use and mental disorders accept and enter outpatient substance abuse treatment.

Encouraged by findings such as these, a transition group was created for clients receiving inpatient alcohol rehabilitation. The hypothesis that guided group design was:

1. If inpatient clients participate in group discussions that sensitize them to specific risks for relapse that they will encounter when they leave the hospital,
2. If they learn alternative, more adaptive responses to use in those high-risk situations, and
3. If they are informed about formal (e.g., alcoholism clinics, Alcoholics Anonymous) and informal (peers, social support networks) resources that support sobriety,
4. Then, they will be more likely to make initial contacts with an outpatient alcoholism clinic,
5. They will maintain active involvement in the clinic, and
6. They will remain abstinent and avoid relapse.

THEORETICAL FRAMEWORK

The transition group's design and development was grounded in three interlocking theoretical and conceptual frameworks: empowerment principles, social learning and self-efficacy theory, and health psychology.

Empowerment Principles. To be empowered means to be masterful and competent so that one can engage in action on her or his own behalf. The empowerment process involves developing attitudes and beliefs about one's capacity to take action, developing a critical grasp of one's world, acquiring the knowledge and skills needed to take action, peer support and mutual aid, and acting to make changes in the face of impinging problems (Parsons, 1991). Empowerment occurs in the context of a supportive social environment in which clients interact and reflect actively with others, "name" the conditions in which they live, and develop problem-posing and decision-making skills that will give them a sense of personal and collective self-efficacy (Freire, 1970; Lee, 1994; Pecukonis & Wenocur, 1994; Simon, 1994; Solomon, 1976). According to Gutierrez and Ortega (1991), "the psychological process of empowerment involves changing the perception of the self in society. This includes the development of a sense of group identity, the reduction of feelings of self blame for problems, an increased sense of responsibility for future events, and enhanced feelings of self-efficacy" (p. 25).

Empowerment principles are particularly useful for working with poor, inner-city residents whose oppressive circumstances adversely affect their self-appraisals and who feel helpless and hopeless in the face of seemingly insurmountable obstacles. Group strategies that facilitate the development of empowerment include constructive dialogues about life events, which help clients learn to question their experiences, and *praxis,* a process of reflecting about, and developing action strategies for, problematic circumstances (Freire, 1973).

Social Learning and Self-Efficacy Theory. Social learning theorists assert that a person's actions are shaped in situational contexts. People are not mechanistically controlled by environmental forces.

Rather, the impact of environmental stimuli is mediated by cognitive processes (Bandura, 1977; Bandura, 1986).

Perceived self-efficacy is one such cognitive process. Essentially, self-efficacy is a performance expectation, a belief that one has the capacity (and right) to exercise control in his or her environment. Perceived self-efficacy is a function of four informational sources: feedback from doing tasks oneself (enactive attainments), vicarious experience, verbal persuasion, and physiological status (biological readiness to act) (Bandura, 1982).

A basic proposition of self-efficacy theory is that people affect their motivational and achievement levels by assessing their ability to cope with specific situational demands (Cervone & Scott, 1995). For example, when individuals encounter high-risk drinking situations they form judgments about the likely outcomes of those situations, as well as their abilities to handle them. If their sense of perceived self-efficacy is low, they will anticipate relapse and they will be less likely to persist in efforts to avoid drinking. If they feel more self-efficacious, they will be more persistent and use a wider variety of strategies to avoid drinking (Annis & Davis, 1988).

The most direct way to influence clients' perceived self-efficacy is to give them opportunities to practice and receive feedback about their use of behavioral change strategies (e.g., Gilchrist, Schinke, Bobo, & Snow, 1986). Thus, if clinicians can help clients identify situations in which they are at-risk for alcohol relapse, develop (and practice) relapse prevention strategies, and receive constructive feedback from peers and treatment staff, their perceived self-efficacy should improve. Correspondingly, they should exert more effort and be more persistent at avoiding relapse when they face threats to their sobriety.

Health Psychology. Health psychologists suggest that for persons to adopt and use preventive and protective behaviors in relapse situations, they must move through several phases (Catania, Kegeles, & Coates, 1990; Rosenstock, Strecher, & Becker, 1988). First, they must be aware of the risks for relapse, they must feel that the risks are serious, and they must feel personally vulnerable for relapse. Second, they must have confidence in resources and responses that are available to prevent relapse. Third, they must have confidence in their own abilities to utilize those resources and responses (i.e., they must feel self-efficacious). Fourth, they must have an opportunity to practice the responses and receive feedback to enhance their abilities to use them. Fifth, they must have the chance to develop and improve their general communication and problem solving skills. Finally, they must believe that the preventive and protective strategies are congruent with their personal values, as well as those of their peers and other social network members.

To be consistent with the principles of health psychology, an effective group program should provide specific information about relapse risks in language the clients can understand. It must provide opportunities for practicing alternative strategies for dealing with pressures to resume drinking. It must promote mutual aid and peer support among the group members.

GROUP STRUCTURE AND PROCESS

The transition group was co-facilitated by two alcoholism counselors, one from the inpatient ward and another from the alcoholism outpatient clinic. Co-facilitators were selected to emphasize the linkages between outpatient and inpatient care and to enable the participants to get a "feel" for the outpatient clinic. Group meetings were held on the ward for 90 minutes each week and were composed of 12 to 16 members depending on the ward's census. All inpatients were required to attend the group.

The leaders combined didactic presentations with participant feedback. The presentations introduced and framed the discussion topics; feedback from the participants about their own life experiences kept the discussions relevant and meaningful. About half of each session was didactic; the other half involved open exchanges about difficult situations that the participants encountered, behavioral rehearsal, and peer feedback.

Each group session covered one of three interrelated topics:

1. Identification of triggers (temptations) in specific high-risk relapse situations.
2. Alternative responses for handling risky situations (including opportunities to practice and receive feedback).

3. Formal and informal resources to support sobriety (e.g., alcohol clinics, Alcoholics Anonymous) and how to use them (e.g., how to get an AA sponsor, how to work with counselors in clinics).

The importance of outpatient continuing care and support in maintaining sobriety was stressed in each group session. Since the average length of stay on the treatment unit was 21 days, each client was able to attend all three group meetings.

The group leaders used several facilitative strategies to enhance the clients' commitment for treatment. Motivational interviewing (Miller & Rollnick, 1991; Rollnick & Morgan, 1995) was employed to help clients recognize and make plans for handling drinking-related problems. For example, through reflective listening, clients were encouraged to elaborate on their prior experiences with alcohol and alcoholism treatment. By posing questions (e.g., "What do you think you were experiencing?" "What do you think you could have done to avoid drinking?") clients were encouraged to reflect critically about their experiences and to consider options for change. With tools like "Decisional Balance Sheets" the members confronted their ambivalences and weighed the costs and benefits of continued drinking, sober lifestyles, and on-going alcoholism treatment (Janis & Mann, 1977; Miller & Rollnick, 1991). The leaders promoted constructive dialogues by actively soliciting members' input and pointing out common themes in their experiences.

Role induction strategies (Zweben, Bonner, Chaim, & Santon, 1988) were used to help group members anticipate and prepare for the demands of outpatient clinics. Group members were "walked through" a typical intake interview. Questions they would be asked were reviewed and their answers were discussed. Doubts they had about remaining sober and continuing in treatment were elicited. Discussions addressed their understanding of the outpatient treatment process, reasons why they might be reluctant to engage in treatment, including any past unpleasant experiences with outpatient treatment, and specific aftercare plans for continuing treatment when they left the hospital.

GROUP SESSIONS

Each group session emphasized one or two intervention components: basic information about risks for relapse, increasing awareness of individual vulnerability and specific risks for relapse, changing beliefs about handling pressures to drink, developing skills for handling pressures to drink, information about available resources, and developing skills to use resources.

Session I. The group leaders explained the group's purpose and clarified its structure with the members. They also provided information about the prevalence of relapse. The group members reacted to this information by sharing personal experiences with relapse and prior unsuccessful strategies they used to maintain sobriety. To increase the participants' sensitivity toward personal risks for relapse, the leaders encouraged them to examine recent specific circumstances in which they drank and the cognitive-behavioral components of those situations (triggers, moods, thoughts, people, consequences). After each member shared, the group leaders reviewed the common triggers and illustrated the multiple associations between drinking, specific social situations, emotional states, and attitudes/beliefs the members held about drinking (McCrady, 1993). The group session concluded with the leaders highlighting that each of them was in "the same boat" and that they needed the help of others to remain sober.

Session II. The second group meeting focussed on skill development. Using the specific high-risk drinking situations that the members identified in the first session, the leaders introduced two fundamental skills: drink refusal and problem-solving.

Since most of the members had difficulty asserting themselves in social situations when friends and relatives pressured them to drink, it was particularly important to help them learn how to refuse drinks. Members learned and role-played a simple five-step process for drink refusal: Acknowledging any request by others to drink; using "I" statements, explicitly declining the offer; stating why one is not drinking; suggesting an alternative activity that does not involve drinking; excusing oneself if the other persons insist on drinking. Throughout this process, participants were encouraged not to attack the other persons or their motives and to focus on themselves and why they were not drinking.

Problem-solving skills, which would minimize the chances that group members would find themselves in high-risk drinking situations, were introduced with the acronym "SODAS," which stands for a five-step decision-making model: Stop (What is the situation? Define the problem and goals); Options (What action alternatives can be generated? Identify the positive and negative consequences associated with each alternative); Decide (After evaluating the alternatives, select one); Act (Implement the decision); and Self-Praise (Reward oneself through internal messages [self-talk] that acknowledge the results) (Gilchrist et al., 1986). Group members practiced decision-making in situations that could lead to drinking (e.g., birthday parties, family gatherings, hanging out with friends). The leaders taught the problem-solving skills by asking members to discuss the strategies they currently used in high-risk drinking situations. Then, by posing questions they helped the entire group evaluate these strategies and select safer alternatives by using the "SODAS" steps. The session ended with the group leaders encouraging members to reflect critically on their experiences and to consider ways they could handle them differently in the future.

Session III. In the last group session, members were helped to identify the different social supports and other resources they could rely on to help them maintain sobriety. Leaders stressed that no one could stay sober alone and that it was important for members to be aware of people, agencies, and support groups they could turn to for support when they were discharged. Members were urged to expand their social networks to include people who were supportive of sobriety and to eliminate (or reduce contact with) people who were threats to their sobriety.

Explicit attention was drawn to the availability of Alcoholics Anonymous and outpatient alcoholism clinics. The leaders explained the philosophies, locations, and structures of different clinics and AA groups. They also encouraged members who had experiences with these organizations to discuss them. The members' comments served as the bases for clarifying members' expectations and concerns about treatment.

The members were given lists of AA meetings and clinic locations. They were encouraged to make telephone calls to connect to AA groups or to re-connect with counselors in alcoholism clinics. Since some members were reluctant to reach out for help, role plays were used to help them practice these strategies and to discuss the feelings evoked in the process. As with the other group sessions, this meeting ended with the group leaders re-iterating that supports were needed and that they were available. It was recommended that members make use of the resources and continue with treatment when they left the hospital.

FINDINGS ABOUT THE GROUP'S EFFECTIVENESS

The transition group's impact on continuity of care was evaluated by reviewing the medical records of all clients referred from the inpatient ward to the outpatient clinic for the 16 months prior to the group's start (n = 93) and the 12 months after the group's implementation (n = 64). We also reviewed the outpatient records of each person who made contact with the clinic to assess that person's status for the six months following admission to the alcoholism clinic. Clients referred to the clinic before the group was implemented were compared to those referred to the clinic after it started in terms of outcomes including their contact rates, lengths of stay, involvement in treatment, and abstinence rates.

The transition group proved to be very effective. After its implementation, the rate of follow-through with outpatient alcoholism treatment improved from 64.5% to 76.6%; the average length of stay in treatment for six months after discharge improved from 16.7 weeks to 20.4 weeks; rates of one-month sobriety at the six month follow-up date improved from 51.7% to 73.5%; and compliance with treatment improved from 43.3% to 75.5% (e.g., clients kept more appointments; they were problem-focused and goal-directed in counseling sessions). The transition group was especially beneficial for persons who were re-admitted to the alcoholism clinic. Re-admitted clients were even more likely than new clients to make contact with the clinic and to establish short-term sobriety. (The reader is referred to Hanson, Foreman, Tomlin, & Bright (1994) for a more in-depth discussion of the transition group's evaluation.)

IMPLICATIONS FOR CLINICAL PRACTICE

The link between inpatient and outpatient alcoholism treatment is a critical one in the treatment process. To mobilize clients so that they will be more likely to make this necessary transition, alcoholism professionals must examine their intervention strategies. Therapeutic outcomes are products of the transactions that occur between clients, significant others, and helping professionals. Clients' responses to helping efforts are, in large part, contingent on what clinicians present to them (Miller & Rollnick, 1991; Shaffer & Robbins, 1995).

This article has described a transition group, which helped inner-city residents completing a hospital-based, inpatient alcoholism rehabilitation make contact with outpatient treatment. It demonstrated that theoretically grounded groups, which focus on the particular tasks clients must master to continue in care, can be effective. The intervention built upon prior clinical efforts. It helped clients identify risks for relapse, develop adaptive responses for handling those risks, and gain confidence and hope that they could avoid relapse. It employed a flexible problem-posing structure that allowed clients to collaborate with counselors in the treatment process and generate solutions that were meaningful for their recovery. This article contributes to the alcoholism treatment knowledge base by showing that modest programmatic changes, which are within a clinical staff's control, can produce beneficial results for clients.

Further study is needed to evaluate more fully the impact of group interventions such as the one described in this paper. The potential benefits of a transition group, which improves the use of continuing outpatient treatment, should stimulate study of similar types of interventions. For example, the critical components of the interventions must be identified, and their generalizability across treatment settings and populations must be examined. The modest treatment gains that were produced by involvement in the transition group illustrate the baffling nature of recovery. The effectiveness of the group, however, should provide hope that responsive interventions can be designed and implemented by utilizing resources that are available in existing alcoholism treatment programs.

REFERENCES

Alterman, A. I., Bedrick, J., Howden, D., & Maany, I. (1994). Reducing waiting time for substance abuse treatment does not reduce attrition. *Journal of Substance Abuse, 6,* 325-332.

Annis, H. M., & Davis, C. S. (1988). Assessment of expectancies. In D. M. Donovan & G. A. Marlatt (Eds.), *Assessment of addictive behaviors* (pp. 84-111). New York: Guilford.

Bandura, A. (1977). Cognitive processes mediating behavior change. *Journal of Personality and Social Psychology, 35,* 125-139.

Bandura, A. (1982). Self-efficacy mechanism in human agency. *American Psychologist, 37,* 122-147.

Bandura, A. (1986). *Social foundations of thought and action: A social cognitive theory.* Englewood Cliffs, NJ: Prentice-Hall.

Castaneda, R. Lifshutz, H., Galanter, M., Medalia, A., & Franco, H. (1992). Treatment compliance after detoxification among highly disadvantaged alcoholics. *American Journal of Drug and Alcohol Abuse, 18,* 223-234.

Catania, J. A., Kegeles, S. M,, & Coates, T. J. (1990). Towards an understanding of risk behavior: An AIDS risk reduction model (ARRM). *Health Education Quarterly, 17,* 53-72.

Cervone, D., & Scott, W. D. (1995). Self-efficacy theory of behavioral change: Foundations, conceptual issues, and therapeutic implications. In W. O'Donohue & L. Krasner (Eds.), *Theories of behavior therapy: Exploring behavior change* (pp. 349-383). Washington, D.C.: American Psychological Association.

Dolan, L.P. (1975). An intake group in the alcoholism outpatient clinic. *Journal of Studies on Alcohol, 36,* 996-999.

Fagan, R. W., & Mauss, A. L. (1986). Social margin and social reentry: An evaluation of a rehabilitation program for skid row alcoholics. *Journal of Studies on Alcohol, 47,* 413-425.

Freire, P. (1970). *Pedagogy of the oppressed.* New York: Continuum.

Freire, P. (1973). *Education for critical consciousness.* New York: Continuum.

Galanter, M., & Panepinto, W. (1980). Entering the alcohol outpatient service: Application of a systems approach to patient drop-out. In M. Galanter (Ed.), *Currents in alcoholism, vol. 7: Recent advances in research and treatment* (pp. 307-313). New York: Grune and Stratton.

Gallant, D. M. (1987). *Alcoholism: A guide to diagnosis, intervention, and treatment.* New York: Norton.

Gilchrist, L. D., Schinke, S. P., Bobo, J. K., & Snow, W. H. (1986). Self-control skills for preventing smoking. *Addictive Behaviors, 11,* 169-174.

Glaser, F. B., Greenberg, S. W., & Barrett, M. (1978). *A systems approach to alcoholism treatment.* Toronto: Addictions Research Foundation.

Gutierrez, L. M., & Ortega, R. (1991). Developing methods to empower Latinos: The importance of groups. *Social Work with Groups, 14*(2), 23-43.

Hanson, M., Foreman, L., Tomlin, W., & Bright, Y. (1994). Facilitating problem drinking clients' transition from inpatient to outpatient care. *Health and Social Work, 19,* 23-28.

Hanson, M., Steward, V., Lundwall, L. K., Higgins, M. J., & El-Bassel, N. (Under review). *Correlates of aftercare attendance by socially disadvantaged alcoholics.*

Institute of Medicine. (1990). *Broadening the base of treatment for alcohol problems.* Washington, DC: National Academy Press.

Ito, J. R., & Donovan, D. M. (1986). Aftercare in alcoholism treatment: A review. In W.R. Miller & N. Heather (Eds.), *Treating addictive behaviors: Processes of change* (pp. 435-456). New York: Plenum.

Janis, I. L., & Mann, L. (1977). *Decision-making: A psychological analysis of conflict, choice, and commitment.* New York: Free Press.

Kirk, S. A., & Masi, J. (1978). Aftercare for alcoholics: Services of community mental health centers. *Journal of Studies on Alcohol, 39,* 545-547.

Kofoed, L., & Keys, A. (1988). Using group therapy to persuade dual-diagnosis patients to seek substance abuse treatment. *Hospital and Community Psychiatry, 39,* 1209-1211.

Lee, J. A. B. (1994). *The empowerment approach to social work practice.* New York: Columbia University Press.

Levinson, V. R. (1979). The decision group: Beginning treatment in an alcoholism clinic. *Health and Social Work, 4,* 199-221.

McCrady, B. S. (1993). Alcoholism. In D. H. Barlow (Ed.), *Clinical handbook of psychological disorders* (2nd ed., pp. 362-395). New York: Guilford.

Miller, W. R., & Rollnick, S. (1991). *Motivational interviewing.* New York: Guilford.

Moos, R. H., & Finney, J. W. (1995). Substance abuse treatment programs and processes: Linkages to patients' needs and outcomes. *Journal of Substance Abuse, 7,* 1-8.

Novick, L. F., Hudson, H., & German, E. (1974). In-hospital detoxification and rehabilitation of alcoholics in an inner-city area. *American Journal of Public Health, 64,* 1089-1094.

Panepinto, W., Galanter, M., Bender, S.H., & Strochlic, M. (1980). Alcoholics' transition from ward to clinic; group orientation improves retention. *Journal of Studies on Alcohol, 41,* 940-945.

Parsons, R. J. (1991). Empowerment: Purpose and practice principle in social work. *Social Work with Groups, 14*(2), 7-21.

Pattison, E. M. (1985). The selection of treatment modalities for the alcoholic patient. In J. H. Mendelson & N. K. Mello (Eds.), *The diagnosis and treatment of alcoholism* (2nd ed., pp. 189-294). New York: McGraw-Hill.

Pecukonis, E. V., & Wenocur, S. (1994). Perceptions of self and collective efficacy in community organization theory and practice. *Journal of Community Practice, 1*(2), 5-21.

Pratt, T. C., Linn, M. W., Carmichael, J. S., & Webb, N. L. (1977). The alcoholic's perception of the ward as a predictor of aftercare attendance. *Journal of Clinical Psychology, 33,* 915-918.

Prochaska, J. O., DiClemente, C. C., & Norcross, J. C. (1992). In search of how people change: Applications to addictive behaviors. *American Psychologist, 47,* 1102-1114.

Rollnick, S., & Morgan, M. (1995). Motivational interviewing: Increasing readiness for change. In A. M. Washton (Ed.), *Psychotherapy and substance abuse: A practitioner's handbook* (pp.179-191). New York: Guilford.

Rosenstock, I. M., Strecher, V. J., & Becker, M. H. (1988). Social learning theory and the health belief model. *Health Education Quarterly, 15,* 175-183.

Shaffer, H. J., & Robbins, M. (1995). Psychotherapy for addictive behavior: A stage-change approach to meaning making. In A. M. Washton (Ed.), *Psychotherapy and substance abuse: A practitioner's handbook* (pp. 103-123). New York: Guilford.

Simon, B. L. (1994). *The empowerment tradition in American social work.* New York: Columbia University Press.

Solomon, B. B. (1976). *Black empowerment.* New York: Columbia University Press.

Stark, M. J. (1992). Dropping out of substance abuse treatment: A clinically oriented review. *Clinical Psychology Review, 12,* 93-116.

Verinis, J. S. (1984). Obtaining alcoholic patient follow-up on aftercare referrals. *Alcohol Health and Research World, 8*(4), 46-47.

Verinis, J. S. (1995). Treatment of the socially disadvantaged alcoholic. *Alcoholism Treatment Quarterly, 12*(2), 93-112.

Verinis, J. S., & Taylor, J. (1994). Increasing alcoholic patients' aftercare attendance. *International Journal of the Addictions, 29,* 1487-1494.

Waisberg, J. L. (1990). Patient characteristics and outcome of inpatient treatment for alcoholism. *Advances in Alcohol and Substance Abuse, 8*(3/4), 9-32.

Zweben, A., Bonner, M., Chaim, G., & Santon, P. (1988). Facilitative strategies for retaining the alcohol-dependent client in outpatient treatment. *Alcoholism Treatment Quarterly, 5*(1/2), 3-23.

An Inpatient Psychoeducational Group Model for Gay Men and Lesbians with Alcohol and Drug Abuse Problems

Joseph H. Neisen, PhD

SUMMARY. This article presents a psychoeducational group model used at Pride Institute, a gay and lesbian affirmative inpatient chemical dependency treatment program. While psychoeducational groups have long been a central component of chemical dependency treatment, gay men and lesbians have extensive treatment needs and these needs may be addressed most effectively in psychoeducational groups that are unique and specific. This model is presented to (1) identify the special needs of chemically dependent gay men and lesbians, (2) raise awareness among treatment providers, (3) apply to other populations that have been marginalized and victimized by majority culture, and (4) be adapted for use by other agencies and treatment programs. *[Article copies available for a fee from The Haworth Document Delivery Service: 1-800-342-9678. E-mail address: getinfo@haworth.com]*

INTRODUCTION

Educational groups have been long considered an essential component of effective alcohol and drug treatment programs (Levine

---

Joseph H. Neisen is President, 18th Street Services/Operation Concern.
Address correspondence to: Dr. Joseph H. Neisen, 18th Street Services, 217 Church Street, San Francisco, CA 94114.

[Haworth co-indexing entry note]: "An Inpatient Psychoeducational Group Model for Gay Men and Lesbians with Alcohol and Drug Abuse Problems." Neisen, Joseph H. Co-published simultaneously in *Journal of Chemical Dependency Treatment* (The Haworth Press, Inc.) Vol. 7, No. 1/2, 1997, pp. 37-51; and: *Chemical Dependency Treatment: Innovative Group Approaches* (ed: L. Donald McVinney) The Haworth Press, Inc., 1997, pp. 37-51. Single or multiple copies of this article are available for a fee from The Haworth Document Delivery Service [1-800-342-9678, 9:00 a.m. - 5:00 p.m. (EST). E-mail address: getinfo@haworth.com].

and Gallogly, 1985; Nace, 1987; Schilit and Gomberg, 1991). Educational workshops provide insights regarding salient clinical issues which can then be addressed within therapy groups. In this sense, educational groups and therapy groups complement each other. An alcohol and drug treatment program utilizing one without the other cannot be effective. Because of the special issues facing gay men and lesbians in today's society, treatment programs that do not provide gay and lesbian individuals with gay/lesbian-specific psychoeducational groups in effect do not provide effective treatment. The result is an increased likelihood that gay and lesbian individuals will not be able to maintain long-term sobriety because they are less likely to be successful in developing skills to (1) accept and affirm their homosexuality, (2) understand the relationship between homophobia/heterosexism and their alcohol/drug abuse and (3) adapt and survive as a gay person in today's world.

Daley (1989) used a psychoeducational model for relapse prevention. This model incorporates educational presentations to assist the individual in developing coping mechanisms to aid in maintaining long term sobriety. These include attitudinal, cognitive and behavioral components. The psychoeducational model utilizes not only educational lecture and discussion groups, but also small and large group tasks.

In addition to the typical psychoeducational groups found in most alcohol and drug treatment programs, such as workshops on cross addiction, the 12 Steps, or relapse prevention, gay and lesbian clients need psychoeducational groups on gay/lesbian issues as they are relevant to and necessary for relapse prevention. In the past, it was standard practice in alcohol and drug treatment centers to focus exclusively on drinking and drugging. This was based on the belief that to discuss other life issues was to "defocus" and that this "defocusing" would jeopardize the primary goal of treatment: to maintain sobriety. For many gay men and lesbians, this meant "you don't need to talk about your sexuality to stay sober." It also frequently meant "we don't want to hear about your homosexuality." Most often, treatment providers were unprepared to address this issue due to their own prejudices, fears and lack of education.

For most gay men and lesbians, this traditional approach to treatment did not work. It did not work because treatment providers were asking gay men and lesbians to separate out a central part of their personhood. With continued societal misinformation and disdain about homosexuality, it was quite common for many gay men and lesbians to arrive in treatment fearful and isolated and filled with shame about their sexual orientation. It was not surprising then, that many of these individuals would go through treatment and never or rarely mention their homosexuality, and ultimately relapse. How could they maintain sobriety when they were still filled with shame about their homosexuality and simultaneously were told it was not an acceptable topic for discussion in treatment?

CHANGING PERSPECTIVES ON HOMOSEXUALITY AND ALCOHOLISM

In the last 15 years, sociocultural influences are more widely recognized as contributing factors to alcohol and drug abuse in gay and lesbian communities. Perspectives have changed regarding both alcoholism and homosexuality. In the past, homosexuality was defined as a mental illness and alcoholism was often treated as a legal problem. Following from the work of Kinsey and his associates (Kinsey, Pomeroy, & Martin, 1948), most informed human service providers presently view homosexuality along a continuum of sexual orientation and define alcoholism and chemical dependency as a disorder characterized by dependency on a psychoactive chemical (American Psychiatric Association, 1994).

Sociocultural explanations for the etiology of addiction are a fairly recent development and were preceded by psychoanalytic theory which linked both homosexuality and alcoholism to incomplete psychosexual development. Nardi (1982) has dispelled the myths regarding the causal relationships between homosexuality and alcoholism and points instead to the need for further investigations using a sociological approach. The psychoanalytic literature has been further reviewed by Israelstam and Lambert (1983; 1986) and they conclusively refute the notion that a latent homosexual drive is the cause of compulsive drinking and drugging. Instead, they explain heavy drinking and drugging by lesbians and gay men as a response to their stigmatization by the dominant culture.

The stigmatization of gay men, lesbians, bisexuals and transgender individuals in our culture is referred to as heterosexism (Neisen, 1990; Neisen, 1993; Neisen, 1994; Heyward, 1992). Heterosexism interferes with emotional growth and development and instills shame. In this culture, individuals are apt to use intoxication of various forms to cope with feelings of shame. Hence, if one is gay, lesbian, bisexual or transgender, drinking or abusing drugs as a means to cope with a hostile social environment may be understandable. For this reason, treatment programs need to address the challenges faced by gay men and lesbians and reduce the shame they feel in order to help them maintain long term sobriety and lead productive and fulfilling lives. Psychoeducational groups for gay men and lesbians serve this purpose.

PSYCHOEDUCATIONAL GROUP GOALS

Psychoeducational groups are both didactic and experiential in nature. Since our society generally provides either no information or misinformation about homosexuality, the first goal of psychoeducational groups for gay men and lesbians is to provide information about what it means to be gay in today's society. Many gay men and lesbians arrive in alcohol and drug treatment programs isolated from any larger gay/lesbian community. This social isolation is a result of both (1) heterosexism and homophobia and (2) alcohol and drug abuse. Gay men and lesbians who have been socially isolated, or perhaps only know other gay men and lesbians within the context of a bar, frequently arrive in treatment having no clear picture of themselves as gay or lesbian, and lack positive connections to gay and lesbian communities. Didactic presentations within psychoeducational groups provide the beginning re-education so that these socially isolated gay men and lesbians are able to re-claim their sexuality and integrate it back into their lives as a central and affirming part of their personhood. Failure to integrate one's sexuality increases the likelihood of relapse as the lingering shame interferes with the self-acceptance necessary for maintaining long term sobriety.

Other gay men and lesbians may enter treatment already possessing a greater level of self-acceptance and community connection. Psychoeducational groups provide these individuals with the opportunity to examine how their addiction has resulted in a diminished capacity to affirm themselves as a gay or lesbian individual and how their alcohol and drug abuse has kept them socially distanced from a positive and constructive larger gay community.

The second goal of psychoeducational groups is to facilitate the integration and personalization of the didactic materials via experiential means. The experiential aspect of psychoeducational groups may consist of (1) small group discussions, (2) large group discussions, (3) question and answer sessions, (4) personal reflections, (5) journaling, (6) art projects, and (7) role plays. The experiential tasks within the psychoeducational groups provide the emotional component of the group. The personalization of the gay/lesbian topics and identification of the emotional aspect of reclaiming one's sexuality and integrating one's sexual orientation provide the basis for therapy groups to further analyze the interrelatedness between loss of identity and addiction.

A GAY- AND LESBIAN-SPECIFIC PSYCHOEDUCATIONAL GROUP MODEL

The psychoeducational group model described here has been developed at Pride Institute in Minneapolis, an inpatient alcohol and drug treatment program specifically designed to meet the needs of gay men and lesbians. Following are several examples of gay/lesbian focused psychoeducational groups.

Session One: Understanding the Connection Between Heterosexism and Addiction

The goals of this psychoeducational group include: (1) recognizing heterosexism as one form of cultural victimization and abuse, (2) understanding how victimization and abuse are connected to alcohol and drug abuse, (3) identification of the harmful effects of heterosexism in the client's personal life, and (4) developing an action plan to heal from the negative effects of heterosexism and live a fulfilling and productive life as a gay, sober and proud individual.

In this group session, clients learn to distinguish between the concepts of homophobia and heterosexism, recognizing the utility of the construct "heterosexism" in framing the prejudice and discrimination they face as one form of cultural victimization, drawing upon parallels with sexism, racism, and classism. This reframing of prejudice as cultural victimization often provides new insights for clients. Clients grew up in a majority culture which told them "there is something wrong with you for being homosexual." The concept of cultural victimization helps clients recognize that this is not about their personhood, but about abuse and victimization. This provides clients with an opportunity to discuss the ways in which heterosexism has contributed to their struggles with self-acceptance, low self-esteem or shame-based identity, anger, and the development of a victim mentality. We then facilitate the connection for clients between these and self-destructive behaviors such as the abuse of alcohol and other drugs. Finally, clients learn that it is possible to effectively negate or minimize these harmful consequences. Each client develops his/her own goals in improving self-image, releasing the shame regarding their homosexuality, affirming and celebrating their sexuality, stopping self-destructive behaviors, and identifying a family or support network that allows them to live their life gay, sober and proud.

Session Two: Coming Out Sober and Alive

There are two primary goals of this psychoeducational group session. First, clients are educated about the various stages of the coming out process (Cass, 1979; Coleman, 1981, 1982) and the risks of alcohol and drug abuse associated with each stage of development. Second, clients learn to recognize the emotional pain of coming out in a heterosexist culture and how this emotional pain, if left unexpressed, may jeopardize attempts to maintain sobriety.

In addition to the presentation of stage models to understand the coming out process, the following kinds of questions are discussed so the client may personally integrate the information:

1. What stage were you in when you started to drink/drug?
2. How have drugs and alcohol affected your movement through the stages of coming out?

3. What are some of the parallels between denial of addiction and denial of sexuality?
4. Is it possible to develop healthy lesbian/gay pride if you are abusing alcohol or other drugs?
5. How will being sober affect your progression through these stages?
6. Are there any stages you will have to do over after achieving sobriety?

Session Three: Gay Men, Lesbians and Spirituality: Silencing the God that Shames

Because many gay men and lesbians have been shunned from religious institutions because of their homosexuality, they frequently arrive in alcohol and drug treatment programs detached from any sense of spirituality. Some religious institutions have in effect stated that it is not possible for gay men and lesbians to be religious or spiritual because homosexuality is perceived as immoral and sinful. This psychoeducational group session helps participants identify the shaming and limiting messages about themselves, God and their sexuality that were instilled by institutional religions and that they grew up with. The goal of the group session is to "silence the God that shames." This involves distinguishing religion from spirituality. Religion is taught. Spirituality is discovered. Individuals are encouraged to develop their own positive and affirming messages about themselves as spiritual beings. For some, this means re-involvement in religious institutions they previously participated in. For example, one gay man stated "I don't like the Catholic Church's current position on homosexuality, but I'm not going to let that stop me from playing an active role in my church. Some day they will stop their bigotry toward lesbians and gays." Yet, others may feel so abused by the religious bigotry they have faced that they reject traditional religious institutions and become involved in gay- and lesbian-affirming churches such as Metropolitan Community Church. Alternatively, they may develop a more personal and individualized spirituality outside of any organized religion. This psychoeducational group session provides participants with the opportunity to discuss these issues as they re-examine spirituality in terms of acceptance, forgiveness, belonging, gratitude, giving back and celebration of life. For many gay men and lesbians, reclaiming spirituality is a necessary component of maintaining sobriety.

Session Four: Growing Up Lesbian and Gay

Most lesbians and gay men grew up feeling isolated and alone because there was no one to talk to who was understanding and accepting about their sexuality. In this group session, individuals discuss how others responded to their sexual orientation, how these responses affected their self-esteem and view of themselves as a lesbian or gay man, and how this affected their alcohol and drug use.

To facilitate discussion, the following questions are used as a guide:

1. How old were you when you realized you were gay or lesbian?
2. What was it like growing up in your family as a gay/lesbian person?
3. What was it like to be gay/lesbian growing up in your community?
4. Who were the first people you told you were gay and how did they respond?
5. How did the responses and actions of others affect your beliefs regarding your homosexuality?
6. How does your belief system contribute to your actions and choices?
7. How have others' responses to your homosexuality, and current and past beliefs about your homosexuality, affected your alcohol and drug use?

Session Five: Gay and Lesbian Couples

This psychoeducational group session focuses on several crucial areas on the topic of gay and lesbian couples. First, individuals are asked to identify the myths and negative stereotypes they learned as children and adolescents about gay and lesbian couples. Because of society's promulgation of negative stereotypes, many gay men and lesbians reach adulthood having accepted these negative stereotypes as fact. This group session may be their first opportunity to critically examine these myths and stereotypes.

The second focus of the session is to discuss the "reality" of gay and lesbian relationships. We help clients identify what is often true about gay and lesbian relationships but rarely discussed, that is that loving, committed partnerships do exist despite society's disapproval and refusal to acknowledge them. There are many fulfilling, healthy and happy families made up of gay men, lesbians, children, and often other extended family members.

Examining the myths versus realities of gay/lesbian relationships sets the stage for further exploration of the "individual issues" each of us brings into relationships, and whether these issues if left unaddressed increase the likelihood that the stereotype or reality comes true. Various issues need to be addressed. These include: (a) Where are you in the coming out process? (b) Where is your partner in the coming out process? (c) What level of comfort do you and your partner have about being gay/lesbian? Relationships that form when one or both individuals are in the early stages of coming out are at increased risk of failing for similar developmental reasons that heterosexual teenage marriages often fail. Unfortunately, gay men and lesbians may blame the demise of their relationships on their sexual orientation, reinforcing the myth that "gay relationships don't work or last" and they may fail to recognize that simply establishing a committed partnership in a stage of development resembling adolescence has inherent risks, whether heterosexual or homosexual.

Finally, relationship issues frequently contribute to relapse. For individuals who are single and in early sobriety, starting a new relationship can jeopardize sobriety by focusing on the relationship. Gay men and lesbians also need to answer questions such as "How will I know when I'm ready to date without risking sobriety?" For gay men and lesbians in committed partnerships, it is also important to re-examine their commitment to one another and to identify the salient issues that support and detract from sobriety, as well as those that support continuation of the couple.

Session Six: Gay/Lesbian Educational Videos

The use of audio/visual materials such as videos can be a useful adjunct to psychoeducational groups. As stated earlier, one of the goals of psychoeducational groups for gay men and lesbians is to help individuals affirm their homosexuality and recognize that self-acceptance is positively correlated with ability to maintain sobriety. There has been a paucity of affirming gay and lesbian images in our culture. Only in the last 15 years has there been a birth of videos that address gay themes hitherto kept from public domain. Even now, there are video documentaries that have not been broadcast by television stations in some communities because gay topics are still seen as "too controversial." Incorporating gay/lesbian video documentaries in alcohol and drug treatment programs can provide an added dimension to help gay men and lesbians discover their rich history as a community, reclaim their personal identity, instill and affirm gay and lesbian pride, and celebrate the diversity within lesbian and gay communities.

Videos such as *The Life of Harvey Milk, Before Stonewall, Pink Triangles, Silent Pioneers,* and the *1993 March on Washington for Lesbian, Gay and Bisexual Rights* are excellent examples of videos that educate gay men and lesbians about their past. Concomitantly, the personal stories within the videos offer portrayals of the courage, tenacity, and pride of numerous gay men and lesbians, each clearly a hero in their own right, as they have faced society's prejudices and discrimination yet claimed their place as proud individuals within the human family.

It is in the processing and discussions following the documentaries that individuals in alcohol and drug treatment are able to relate their personal struggles. Thus, the videos provide another opportunity to emotionally connect individuals to their community. After years of silence, combined with drug and alcohol abuse, gay men and lesbians are able to identify the importance of and strategize how they will stay connected with their community as a means of maintaining both pride and sobriety.

Implications for Other Treatment Programs: Developing a Culturally Sensitive versus a Culturally Affirming Treatment Program

"Culturally sensitive" and "Culturally specific" programs are increasing in numbers as alcohol and drug treatment providers attempt to meet the clinical needs of diverse populations. It is imperative for alcohol and drug treatment providers to continue to create programs that can address the impact of cultural victimization in order to meet the needs of minority populations that our dominant culture continues to stigmatize and marginalize. Programmatically, treatment providers need to help clients identify: (1) how cultural victimization (heterosexism, racism, classism, and sexism) contributes to substance abuse; (2) how cultural victimization creates shame that interferes with an individual's ability to achieve and maintain sobriety; and (3) how they can begin to release their shame and reclaim their pride as gay men and lesbians in order to maximize their ability to lead fulfilling and productive lives in recovery.

Chemical dependency treatment providers need to distinguish between the concepts of "culturally sensitive" and "culturally specific." They must ask themselves: (1) how culturally sensitive is our practice/program? and (2) do we want to and are we able to implement a culturally specific program?

Because most providers work with heterogeneous client populations, it is important that all treatment providers become more culturally competent and improve their skills in providing culturally sensitive counseling. All treatment providers need to establish some minimum standards of sensitivity so that all clients, regardless of age, race, ethnicity, sexual orientation, gender, and socio-economic status feel safe, respected and supported. In traditional, mainstream, non-culturally specific treatment programs, it is common to find tremendous diversity among clients so that sensitivity to the needs of all individuals is an ongoing issue. At the same time, challenges exist even in culturally specific treatment programs such as Pride Institute, where programs designed to meet the special needs of gay men and lesbians face ongoing issues of maintaining standards of cultural sensitivity. It is important for chemical dependency treatment providers to remember that there is not one monolithic gay community, but rather diverse communities of gay men and lesbians who are young and old, white and black, Latino/a, Asian/Pacific Islander, Native American, professional/non-professional, and in rural, suburban, and urban areas.

As treatment providers improve their cultural sensitivity to meet the needs of clients, a frequently asked question may be whether or not to establish a culturally specific program that will also be culturally sensitive. It may be helpful for providers to identify levels of cultural sensitivity and specificity along a continuum that could be used to clarify program goals and objectives.

The following continuum model focuses on gay-specific programming, although parallels may be drawn with other special populations (see Tables 1a and b).

TABLE 1a.

Anti-Gay Treatment Providers	Traditional Treatment Providers	Gay-Naive Treatment Providers	Gay-Tolerant Treatment Providers
No Gay Sensitivity	No Gay Sensitivity	No Gay Sensitivity	Minimal Gay Sensitivity
Antagonistic toward gays	Don't realize they have gay clients	Realize that they have had gay clients	Currently recognize they have gay/lesbian clients
Treatment program focus is exclusively for heterosexuals and deliberately excludes gays and lesbians	No acknowledgement or discussion of gays Everyone is assumed to be heterosexual	As an agency have not yet begun to address the special issues gays and lesbians face	Some staff may verbalize to clients that it's okay to be gay, however, discussions about being gay usually happen in individual sessions as concerns remain as to "how the group would handle a gay person." No defined plan or policy as to how the staff would deal with homophobic and heterosexist comments/ actions
No specific gay treatment components	No specific gay treatment components	No specific gay treatment components	No specific gay treatment components

TABLE 1b.

Gay-Sensitive	Gay-Affirming
Moderate Level Sensitivity	Highest Level Sensitivity
Several clients and/or staff are open about their homosexuality	All treatment workshops, groups are designed specifically for gay, lesbian, bisexual and transgender individuals
May have several workshops and/or groups focusing on gay/lesbian issues	Therapy groups and workshops are never mixed with heterosexual groups
May have some groups specifically for gays/lesbians	All workshops move beyond gay sensitivity, but affirm the gay, lesbian, bisexual and transgender individual
May be a "track" program that does some gay-specific groups but, also has gay clients mixed with the general facility population in other groups	Workshops on addiction issues incorporate special issues facing gays and lesbians Special workshops on gay and lesbian issues always tie back to sobriety issues Treatment program has gay/lesbian magazines/newspapers available. Posters and other images of the lesbian/gay communities are displayed throughout the treatment building
Some gay-specific treatment components	All treatment components gay-specific

Various points are identified on the continuum from anti-gay treatment providers to gay-affirming treatment providers. There can also be a wide degree of sensitivity/lack of sensitivity at each point identified. The utility of the continuum is to help treatment providers recognize the differences between levels of care, between cultural sensitivity and cultural specificity. In establishing treatment programs, providers can use this continuum to clarify their goals and philosophy as an agency, and then accurately inform prospective clients about the kind of services provided, including the level of cultural sensitivity and cultural specificity.

This article has presented a psychoeducational group model used at Pride Institute, an inpatient chemical dependency treatment program. While psychoeducational groups have long been a central component of chemical dependency treatment, gay men and lesbians have extensive treatment needs and these needs may be addressed most effectively in psychoeducational groups that are unique and specific. This model is presented to (1) identify the special needs of chemically dependent gay men and lesbians, (2) raise awareness among treatment providers, (3) apply to other populations that have been marginalized and victimized by majority culture, and (4) be adapted for use by other agencies and treatment programs.

REFERENCES

American Psychiatric Association. (1994). *Diagnostic and statistical manual of mental disorders.* Fourth Edition. Washington, DC: American Psychiatric Association.

Cass, V. (1979). Homosexual identity formation: A theoretical model. *Journal of Homosexuality, 4,* 219-235.

Coleman, E. (1981-1982). Developmental stages of the coming out process. *Journal of Homosexuality, 7* (2/3), 31-43.

Daley, D. (1989). A psychoeducational approach to relapse prevention. *Journal of Chemical Dependency Treatment, 2*(2), 105-124.

Heyward, C. (1992). Healing addiction and homophobia: Reflections on empowerment and liberation. In D. Weinstein (Ed.), Lesbians and gay men: Chemical dependency issues. Special issue of *Journal of Chemical Dependency Treatment, 5*(1), 5-18.

Israelstam, S. & Lambert, S. (1983). Homosexuality as a cause of alcoholism: A historical review. *International Journal of the Addictions, 18*(8).

Israelstam, S. & Lambert, S. (1986). Homosexuality and alcohol: Observations and research after the psychoanalytic era. *International Journal of the Addictions, 21*(4/5), 509-537.

Kinsey, A. C., Pomeroy, W. B., & Martin, C. E. (1948). *Sexual behavior in the human male.* Philadelphia, PA: W. B. Saunders Company.

Levine, B. & Gallogly, V. (1985). *Group therapy with alcoholics: Outpatient and inpatient approaches.* Beverly Hills, CA: Sage Publications.

Nace, E. (1987). *The treatment of alcoholics.* New York: Brunner/Mazel Publishers.

Nardi, P. (1982). Alcoholism and homosexuality: A theoretical perspective. *Journal of Homosexuality, 7*(1), 9-25.

Neisen, J. H. (1990). Heterosexism: Redefining homophobia for the 1990s. *Journal of Gay & Lesbian Psychotherapy, 1*(3), 21-35.

Neisen, J. H. (1993). Healing from cultural victimization: Recovery from shame due to heterosexism. *Journal of Gay & Lesbian Psychotherapy, 2*(1), 49-63.

Neisen, J. H. (1994). *Counseling lesbian, gay and bisexual persons with alcohol and drug abuse problems.* Arlington, VA: NAADAC Education and Research Foundation.

Schilit, R. & Gomberg, E. (1991). *Drugs and behavior: A sourcebook for the helping professions.* Newbury Park, CA: Sage Publications.

A Hospital-Based
Early Recovery Group Program
for HIV-Infected Inner-City Clients:
Engagement Strategies

Curtis J. Brown, CSW

SUMMARY. This article will present the various strategies used to develop a support group program which engages inner-city clients who are in early recovery from chemical dependence and infected with HIV. The article will also emphasize how assessing and possessing an in-depth understanding of the needs of clients is a prerequisite to planning and conducting successful group treatment. This article also suggests that maintaining abstinence in recovery from chemical dependency and preventing relapse are critical to the management of HIV infection as a chronic illness. This group model is an outgrowth of ongoing work at Gouverneur Hospital, Department of Psychiatry, Ryan White Mental Health Linkage Program in New York City. *[Article copies available for a fee from The Haworth Document Delivery Service: 1-800-342-9678. E-mail address: getinfo@haworth.com]*

BACKGROUND

Gouverneur is an out-patient diagnostic and treatment center (DTC) operated by the New York City Health and Hospital Corpo-

---

Curtis Brown is Director, AIDS Mental Health Program, Gouverneur Hospital, New York, NY.

[Haworth co-indexing entry note]: "A Hospital-Based Early Recovery Group Program for HIV-Infected Inner-City Clients: Engagement Strategies." Brown, Curtis J. Co-published simultaneously in *Journal of Chemical Dependency Treatment* (The Haworth Press, Inc.) Vol. 7, No. 1/2, 1997, pp. 53-65; and: *Chemical Dependency Treatment: Innovative Group Approaches* (ed: L. Donald McVinney) The Haworth Press, Inc., 1997, pp. 53-65. Single or multiple copies of this article are available for a fee from The Haworth Document Delivery Service [1-800-342-9678, 9:00 a.m. - 5:00 p.m. (EST). E-mail address: getinfo@haworth.com].

53

ration on the Lower East Side of Manhattan. In 1992, the hospital received Ryan White CARE Act, Title I, funding to develop a linkage program to address the mental health needs of targeted "hard-to-reach" HIV+ individuals and to provide technical assistance on mental health issues to community-based organizations (CBOs) on the Lower East Side.

POPULATION

Of the clients we serve in group treatment, approximately 75% are African-American, 15% are Hispanic, 5% are African-Caribbean, and 5% are Caucasian gay men. Males comprise 80% of the group membership, 20% are female. Most of the clients are in their 30s or 40s. Group members have extensive histories of chemical dependency, including histories of injection drug use. Most clients attending groups are in early recovery. Many clients have recently graduated from residential treatment programs, notably therapeutic communities, and also attend twelve-step programs, especially Narcotics Anonymous. A few clients participate in methadone maintenance treatment programs. Our clients report drug and alcohol use across all classifications of psychoactive substances beginning as early as 10 or 11 years of age, and almost all of our clients have injected heroin.

Most of the clients have had periods of incarceration, mostly for lower-level street crimes and drug-related offenses. In addition, a number of the clients have had unstable, often chaotic, housing including periods of homelessness and routine contact with the shelter system. Many of the clients have had minimal educational opportunities and state that they aspire to complete a high school equivalency exam at a later point in life.

Other than managing active chemical dependence or addiction, few of the clients have had other experiences with management of a chronic medical condition such as HIV. Clients have said their typical contact with the medical establishment has solely been in an emergency room for treatment of a gunshot or knife wound or for a drug overdose. A basic mistrust of public institutions is prevalent. With regard to HIV and the etiology of AIDS, most clients believe in various conspiracy theories, including that HIV was developed by the U. S. government to rid the nation of less desirable individuals, such as themselves.

From a clinical perspective, many of the clients manifest features commonly associated with chemical dependency, including impulsivity, low frustration tolerance, and the need for immediate gratification. Many of the clients employ manipulative styles of relating. A number of clients also meet DSM-IV criteria for various personality disorders including Borderline, Narcissistic and Schizoid Personality Disorders (American Psychiatric Association, 1994). A percentage of clients have also had more severe psychiatric conditions such as thought or mood disorders. Approximately 20% of the clients have acted on previous suicidal ideation. In addition, many of the clients have experienced adjustment reactions, including anxiety and depression, after learning of their HIV diagnosis. It is not surprising that features of Post-Traumatic Stress Disorder (PTSD) are also present given the psychosocial histories experienced by clients. Those histories include many instances of extreme emotional, physical and/or sexual abuse.

Unlike clients in other psychiatric clinics in our hospital who are motivated and invested in their treatment as a major part of their life experience, most of our clients are quite reluctant to identify with this population out of fear of being labeled or stigmatized. Most are highly resistant to any form of mental health treatment. They usually have little understanding of what treatment means other than that other people will think they are crazy.

CLINICAL IMPLICATIONS FOR GROUP PLANNING

Group treatment is generally regarded as the treatment of choice for chemically dependent or addicted individuals (Golden, Khantzian & McAuliffe, 1994). After exploring various group treatment approaches, our program has been able to successfully develop and sustain 11 weekly drop-in support groups that address early recovery, relapse prevention, and issues related to HIV. We initially adopted a pre-existing model developed by a CBO for people with HIV involved in our linkage program. This CBO model was successful in training and supervising volunteers who were themselves infected with HIV to run groups as "peer-facilitators." The model consisted of closed, short-term psychoeducational groups which met for twelve sessions and focused almost entirely on HIV issues. This model was originally developed by members of the gay community to address the psychosocial needs of HIV-infected gay men.

When our program began offering this particular CBO group model to men of color, to mothers, and other clients who were HIV+, little interest was shown and few, if any, attended group. In addition, we had a difficult time getting peer-facilitators to consistently attend since their lives were often unstable. Our next step was to further assess the needs of our clients in order to inform our group planning process.

A more thorough assessment of the psychosocial pressures of our clients helped us to understand why it was difficult for peer-facilitators who represented our client population to often fulfill their commitment to lead weekly meetings. A mother who led the Mothers Group, for example, had a daughter who had resumed drug use and dropped off her 2-year-old granddaughter with the peer facilitator. This occurred soon after the death of the facilitator's mother. Of course, it is not surprising that she dropped out of sight and left her role as facilitator of the group. Since she did not have a telephone we did not hear of her crisis or anticipate the need for finding her replacement.

Although peer facilitators are often our most stable clients, they found it difficult to follow through on group responsibilities. Given this experience, it did not appear that continuing to offer our clients an on-going, closed group was realistic. Next, we conceptualized "drop-in" groups. A flyer was developed which thoroughly explained the meaning of our groups: what they are and what they are not, including the benefits of sharing in a group. We also insured that confidentially would be maintained. Still no one came.

We next strategized providing incentives for the clients to attend a group. After months of negotiating with an administrator over whether serving a meal was appropriate, we were finally given permission to provide lunches to group members. We began inviting clients to what we called "lunch meetings," although these meetings were, in fact, support groups. No mention of "group" was made, and finally a few clients trickled in to check out the lunch offer. The time period was also convenient for clients, since we had done an assessment and found that the hospital's HIV clinic was closed during lunch hour and clients had often been seen wandering throughout the hospital with no plans for that hour.

This new modality of offering group support at a lunch-time drop-in meeting finally appeared to be effective. In our first week, Jorge, for example, reluctantly attended a lunch meeting. Typical of many of our clients, Jorge had tested HIV+ a year earlier. He had decided to be tested at the urging of our emergency room doctor who had examined Jorge's scalp which was found to be covered in AIDS-related eczema. After testing HIV+, Jorge's first T-cell test revealed that he had 3 T-cells remaining. Both of these factors (the eczema and low T-cell count) suggest that Jorge's HIV infection had been progressing significantly over a number of years. It is likely that Jorge's previous anxiety about being HIV-infected and avoidant about being tested resulted in the use of denial to cope with his physical symptoms.

In the group, Jorge was an active listener and began to participate more and more. Towards the end of group Jorge asked another member how he had worked through so much denial. The other member said he regularly attended support groups. Jorge's response was that he would never attend a group nor did he believe that they were valuable. Of course, unbeknownst to Jorge, he was sitting in a group. Jorge became familiar with the lunch meetings, befriended other clients, and has continued to attend regularly and receive support.

Programmatically, one of the next major changes that we implemented to further engage clients was to increase the frequency of the groups offered. Further assessment of our clients' needs revealed that clients would be interested in attending a group if it was available "right now." While they would be genuinely interested in the next group scheduled for later in the week, by the time the group actually occurred they would have lost interest. A higher frequency of group programming helped us to increase attendance since clients often lived in adjacent boroughs and would travel an hour or two in order to protect their confidentiality. The clients simply did not return for a group scheduled on another day, despite their stated motivation to do so.

We found that by increasing the frequency of groups, we created more momentum. Most days offered between two or three groups which addressed the clients' need for immediacy. It is not unusual that the clients would visit as many groups as possible when they were in crisis or feeling susceptible to relapse. Unlike other communities, our clients did not have the social supports or back-up that would allow them to wait to return to a closed group a week later. While delaying gratification or increasing frustration tolerance is a good treatment goal, we found immediate availability of treatment is appropriate when clients are so prone to relapse.

Yalom states that although it is usually difficult to assemble out-patient groups more frequently than twice a week, it is, in fact, very effective for the group (Yalom, 1975). He explains that the group suffers from the long interval between sessions if it meets once a week:

> Often much that cannot be ignored has occurred in the lives of the members; and the group has a tendency to veer away from interaction into crisis resolution. When the group meets more than once a week, it increases in intensity, the members continue to work through issues raised the previous week, and the entire process takes on the character of a continuous meeting. (Yalom, 1975, p. 278)

It has also appeared that increasing the frequency of groups makes it easier for clients to conceptualize the value of a group. As one group member stated, "When you're stressed and out of control you drop in on a group." The more schizoid client feels safer in having to make less of a commitment to a drop-in group and therefore does not have to wrestle with issues of dependency that arise with a closed group. Clients seem to also have less issues around a mental health stigma in the daily drop-in groups. Overall, the drop-in groups appear more real and "here and now" for the clients. So again, while a treatment goal might have clients face dependency fears, we have based our program design on what we believed the clients could tolerate and on what would help in preventing relapse.

Another advantage of offering a high frequency of drop-in groups is that it provides an opportunity for the groups to become more cohesive. The group members appear to gain closeness as a problem moves through the groups and the members participate in responding to an individual member's problems. The high frequency also helps the clients deal with one of the main obstacles to maintaining sobriety: isolation. Many clients have begun to use the groups in a manner similar to a day-program. The groups provide them with regular contact with people who are clean, supportive and understanding of their struggles and issues. The group is also empowering when clients are able to help a client newly diagnosed as HIV+ or who is feeling "urges" to resume substance use.

CURRENT GROUP EXPERIENCE

The Ryan White Program is involved in five daily lunch groups, two early recovery groups, a peer-facilitated evening group, another peer group held off-site in a therapeutic community, an evening group, a movie/socialization group, and a yoga/stress management group. Depending on the need, we have also had a mentally ill/ chemically addicted (MICA) group for more psychiatrically severe clients. With the exception of the peer groups, all groups are co-led by clinicians from the hospital. Four psychology interns from our APA-approved program participate as co-leaders.

Two important principles are used in planning and conducting our group program. The first is that chemical dependency is viewed as the primary illness in the HIV+ client when both factors exist. The second is that the basis for planning or conducting the group is based on what the client will tolerate.

First, it is clear that maintaining abstinence dramatically improves our clients' likelihood of realistically participating in the rigorous process of managing HIV infection as a chronic illness. Management of medication, nutrition, and other potentially life-sustaining practices often lose priority once the client resumes drug use. Clients who are actively drinking and drugging are much more likely to miss appointments with HIV care providers and the staff at entitlement programs for financial assistance and housing. Illness or substantial psychosocial pressures, such as loss of housing or income, will often occur after missing these types of appointments.

Second, much of the preceding discussion demonstrates the need to understand client needs in the planning stage. It is necessary to be equally responsive to the needs of clients in facilitating the groups.

One area of learning is the active stance we take with clients participating in group. An active leadership style from facilitators provides structure which represents safety for clients who often lead chaotic and/or threatening lives. The leaders provide limit setting, enforce group rules, and provide an environment safe from acting-out behavior. Kantzian, Halliday and McAuliffe (1990) report that:

> addicted individuals with histories of neglect and trauma do not respond well to the traditions of therapeutic passivity . . . instead they need therapists who can actively and empathetically help to engage them and each other around their vulnerabilities and the self-defeating defenses and behaviors they adopt to avoid their distress and suffering. (p. 162)

In fact, our clients do not appear to understand a more reserved or traditional psychoanalytic stance to treatment. An attempt to maintain typical therapeutic boundaries is often misconstrued by our clients as hostile or withholding.

From a theoretical perspective, we have used the Modified Dynamic Group Therapy model (Khantzian, Halliday & McAuliffe, 1990). The authors suggest that the Modified Dynamic Group Therapy (MDGT) model specifically addresses the needs and problems of the chemically dependent individual. They believe that the client's vulnerabilities can be conceptualized into four main categories of experience: (1) accessing, tolerating, and regulating of feelings, (2) problems with relationships, (3) self-care failures, and (4) self-esteem deficits.

Undoubtedly, one of the areas of feelings that our clients struggle with is their HIV status. The issues of loss from such factors as death, resumption of drug-use, or a drop in t-cells have a chilling effect on the group. Clients have tremendous difficulty acknowledging the impact that HIV has on their lives. For example, one patient, Ebony, an African American female, becomes angry and confrontational as her illness progresses. She can become hostile when group members or facilitators ask her to look at her intense feeling of loss or anxiety of facing death. Surely, some of her historic self-destructive coping patterns and conflicts are revived when such intense feelings about death and loss are denied so vehemently.

Clients' experiences of developing relationships, the second part of the MDGT model, varies significantly among our clients. Often, most of the clients' previous relationships have been with other chemically dependent people who share drug use experiences. The client is then faced with beginning new friendships and relationships, a critical part of maintaining their sobriety. For the more schizoid clients, simply asking for a telephone number in order to establish a new relationship is overwhelming and fraught with concerns about rejection. Other clients may use the group as a source of dating partners while inevitably showing the rest of the group how dating multiple partners has replaced drug use as a compulsive or addictive behavior. The groups often appear similar to an adolescent school yard field when members report back their sexual escapades or conquests. Other clients are narcissistically vulnerable when asking out a potential partner since it is a new experience as someone who is recently "clean" and HIV+. Many group members report on issues of impotency or other sexual performance problems which appear to be displayed anxiety about the fears of rejection or lack of self-esteem.

The case of Frank is a good example. At 38 years old, he has never had more than 6 months clean from one form of drug use or another since his early teenage years. He recently graduated after six months in a Therapeutic Community. Even birthdays and holidays carry special weight and stress for him since many are the first he has ever experienced clean. While he had numerous sexual encounters while he was on the street or with girlfriends who were also active addicts, Frank has never dated someone while clean. He clearly uses the help and support of the group to help him through these difficult times.

In terms of self-care, a sense of omnipotence often has the more schizoid clients with addictive disorders reluctant to depend on one another for help (Seinfeld, 1990). The client's ability to anticipate the anxiety of a situation and exercise appropriate judgement on issues of self-care is impaired by the client's belief that he or she can handle anything. Much of the group's time is spent asking the client to anticipate or project the affect that might accompany a situation. Clients are often asked to look at the degree to which drug-dependent features could be influencing their motivation.

The client Henry illustrates many of these issues. He was serving prison time for a felony drug-related crime. He agreed to enter a therapeutic community for an earlier release from prison. The TC was a fairly lenient program compared to many. While in prison, Henry had tested HIV+ but remained asymptomatic. With two months remaining in his program, he began to attend our drop-in support groups at the hospital. During this time he began to look at housing options for when he completed his program. He was quite impulsive in accepting the first housing offered to him. He often stated that any place would be better than where he was. Henry could not see or acknowledge that there could be stress in this type of move; it was difficult for him to anticipate the issues that could arise. He interpreted most attempts by staff members to have him look at the consequences of his behavior as comments that undervalued his ability to survive. Group members were a little more helpful but still most were very reserved, believing that they would be holding him back by voicing their concerns.

Initially Henry did well but floundered when dealing with the lack of structure he was accustomed to during incarceration or in drug treatment. Both places had given him a reason to exist, mostly to fight the injustice and to dream of the outside. However, it was difficult for him to anticipate the day-to-day stressors of the outside world. Since Henry had been impatient to leave, the apartment he found was in a "crack house" where drug use was prevalent. Given the environmental stimuli, his difficulty in dealing with isolation, and the lack of structure in his life, Henry soon relapsed.

Most of this case material above also provides examples of self-esteem deficits, the fourth part of the MDGT model. Issues of low self-esteem are discussed often in the groups.

GROUP STRUCTURE AND CHARACTERISTICS

A number of rules have developed as the groups have progressed. The rules help to provide structure and a safe environment. We have also observed a number of characteristics of the drop-in groups which differ from experiences in closed groups. We generally run groups with four agreed rules: (1) there is no "nodding off," sleeping, or attending the meeting under the influence of psychoactive substances; (2) clients should arrive on time and stay until the end of group; (3) clients may not attack other group members either physically or verbally; and (4) group discussions must remain confidential.

With the exception of "nodding off," most of the rules are self-explanatory. Clients "nodding off" or coming to the meetings under the influence evokes strong reactions from recovering clients and staff. Clients who are "nodding off" for whatever reasons (methadone or lack of sleep) are typically not confronted but asked to come back another day. "Nodding off" usually occurs when clients are still intoxicated from substance use, including methadone. Understandably, many abstinent clients experience envy and rage at another client who is perceived to be "enjoying" the feeling of intoxication while they struggle to stay clean. Often, they are reluctant to address these feelings directly in the group.

In general, we have found that group members are reluctant to confront one another in a drop-in group format. Unlike closed groups, the usual safety of knowing group members well enough to be confrontive is often absent with drop-in groups. It has been difficult to even have group members discuss the reasons why the most mild confrontation is difficult for them. However, it appears that some clients are accustomed to physical threats to their safety when they confront one another on the street. Also, since most clients are people of color and most of the staff are not, racial issues may play a significant role in the client's unwillingness to join the confrontation by a staff member "against" a peer.

Monopolizing is another example of behavior which clients are reluctant to address. Clients will bitterly complain outside of the group about a monopolizer but even after encouragement will be reluctant to state so in a group. In general, it has been difficult for facilitators to mobilize much feedback or comment on a monopolizer's impact on the group.

The group also attracts many "help rejecting complainers" (Yalom, 1975). These type of clients will often show up after a long "run" of drug use. Much of the group time will be used to rescue this client, only to see the client reject any real help. The help rejecting complainer is more invested in seeing the plight of the world as so overwhelming that s/he cannot be held accountable for accepting any responsibility for his or her own life. Other group members often enjoy the feeling of being empowered by reciting the success of their treatment or standard twelve-step jargon while attempting to rescue the "help rejecting complainers." Of course, if this group dynamic is not interpreted or explained, the group sooner or later grows impatient and angry at the "help rejecting complainer" who then feels rejected, which then justifies the resumption of drug use. This type of client will use the group to confirm that no one really cares about them.

Flores (1988) provides an extensive discussion on confronting the resistances of alcoholic group members which we have found to be a helpful approach. He reviews the various defenses developed by the individual which grow more rigid and maladaptive over time. He describes the need for confrontation which "calls a spade a spade in a realistic fashion without adopting a punitive, moralistic or superior attitude" (p. 287). Johnson (1973) adds that confrontations should not be an attack on the individual but instead a "description of the other person made in a way as is most likely to be received by him" (p. 116).

STAFF ISSUES

A number of staff issues have arisen as this program was developed. We have found that a peer process group for co-leaders of the groups has been important. We meet weekly for one hour to review the week's work. The group helps to provide a sense of continuity around whatever issues or changes have occurred in clients in the various groups they might have attended during the week.

It also is helpful for the staff to feel supported in their work with clients who can be aggressive or difficult to work with. Support is also important for the helplessness and hopelessness often felt by staff members with clients who are experiencing loss through illness, death and relapse. The staff has felt safe in working through any number of countertransferential feelings in response to the clients.

The peer process group has also helped staff to address the differences in the facilitation style of the various co-leaders. This discussion has been especially helpful since we have had to redefine many of the traditional boundaries of a group.

CONCLUSION

A thorough understanding of the psychosocial issues and needs of the clients is a prerequisite to effectively engaging them in treatment. This is especially true for inner-city, chemically dependent, HIV+ clients who have been previously thought of as "difficult to engage." This article suggests that an understanding of these clients coupled with flexible planning and facilitating can provide a meaningful experience for both the client and group therapist.

REFERENCES

American Psychiatric Association. (1994). *Diagnostic and statistical manual of mental disorders* (4th ed.). Washington, D.C.: American Psychiatric Association.

Flores, P. (1988). *Group psychotherapy with addicted populations.* New York: The Haworth Press, Inc.

Golden, S., Khantzian, E., & McAuliffe, W. (1994). *Group therapy. Textbook of substance abuse treatment.* Washington, D.C.: American Psychiatric Press.

Johnson, V. (1973). *I'll quit tomorrow.* New York: Harper & Row.

Khantzian, E., Halliday, & McAuliffe, W. (1990). *Addiction and the vulnerable self.* New York: Guilford Press.

Seinfeld, J. (1991). *The empty core.* Northvale, NJ: Jason Aronson.

Yalom, I. D. (1975). *The theory and practice of group psychotherapy.* New York: Basic Books.

Group Treatment
with Substance Abusing Clients:
A Model of Treatment
During the Early Phases
of Outpatient Group Therapy

Shulamith Lala Ashenberg Straussner, DSW

SUMMARY. Group treatment is frequently viewed as treatment of choice for people abusing or addicted to alcohol and other drugs (substance abusers). The purpose of this paper is to discuss the dynamics of substance abusers and present a model of treatment during the early phases of outpatient group therapy. *[Article copies available for a fee from The Haworth Document Delivery Service: 1-800-342-9678. E-mail address: getinfo@haworth.com]*

Group treatment is frequently viewed as treatment of choice for people abusing, or addicted to, alcohol and/or other drugs, hereby

Shulamith Lala Ashenberg Straussner is Associate Professor, New York University School of Social Work, 1 Washington Square North, New York, NY 10003. The author is also a private practitioner, supervisor and consultant in New York City.

The author would like to thank Drs. Sondra Brandler, Joel Straussner and Scott Davidson for their helpful review of this paper.

This paper is based on a presentation at The Israeli Congress on Group Therapy, March 16, 1994, Tel Aviv, Israel, and was written while the author was Visiting Professor, Bob Shapell School of Social Work, Tel Aviv University.

[Haworth co-indexing entry note]: "Group Treatment with Substance Abusing Clients: A Model of Treatment During the Early Phases of Outpatient Group Therapy." Straussner, Shulamith Lala Ashenberg. Co-published simultaneously in *Journal of Chemical Dependency Treatment* (The Haworth Press, Inc.) Vol. 7, No. 1/2, 1997, pp. 67-80; and: *Chemical Dependency Treatment: Innovative Group Approaches* (ed: L. Donald McVinney) The Haworth Press, Inc., 1997, pp. 67-80. Single or multiple copies of this article are available for a fee from The Haworth Document Delivery Service [1-800-342-9678, 9:00 a.m. - 5:00 p.m. (EST). E-mail address: getinfo@haworth.com].

67

referred to as substance abusers (for fuller definition of terms see Straussner, 1993). Group treatment for substance abusers allows for positive peer interactions, improvement in communication skills, mutual support, confrontation of ego syntonic behaviors and idealization of those who maintain recovery from drugs and alcohol. It has even been suggested that groups substitute the elation of the group for the euphoric state of intoxication (Cooper, 1987; Flores, 1988; Vanicelli, 1992).

In spite of the current emphasis on short term, behavioral treatment, recovery from substance abuse is a long term process and many clinicians are leading long-term groups. Such treatment, however, must vary in content and process during the different phases of recovery and of group stages. The purpose of this paper is to explore the dynamics of substance abusers and to discuss the implications of these dynamics for early phases of outpatient group treatment.

PSYCHODYNAMICS OF SUBSTANCE ABUSERS

In order to provide appropriate treatment, the group leader must have some understanding of the psychodynamics of substance abusing individuals since such dynamics affect the kinds of treatment approaches needed by these group members.

Although numerous theories of personality and of etiologies of substance abuse or addictions can be found in the literature (see Straussner, 1993), group therapists may find it useful to view substance abusers as individuals for whom drugs and alcohol become a substitute for other objects, or people, in addition to providing a temporary relief from psychic pain. At the same time, it is important to keep in mind that the chemical effect of drugs and alcohol leads to the use of more primitive defensive operations such as denial, splitting, projective identification and grandiosity.

These secondary defenses, although providing a protective shield, have the negative consequence of further impairing object relations and isolating the substance abuser from meaningful contact with others. Such impairment frequently leads to further feelings of distrust, anger, deprivation, emptiness, isolation and susceptibility to narcissistic injury. Moreover, due to a combination of pathological development as well as the chemical effects of drugs and alcohol, the substance abuser may exhibit various defects in other ego functions such as reality testing, judgment, stimulus barrier, and regulation and control of drives, affects and impulses (Khantzian, Halliday & McAuliffe, 1990).

Consequently, substance abusers often show disturbances in interpersonal relationships, as well as in their self care. They lack the ability to use signal anxiety and to protect themselves from internal chaos. Due to defects in stimulus barrier, they are frequently unable to modulate their feelings and either over-react or under-react to feeling states. Frequently, they are unable to identify affects such as anger, anxiety or depression and tend to deal with sensations rather than feeling states. Those feelings are then translated into somatic complaints about physical discomfort and craving (Flores, 1988).

As this very brief description of dynamics indicates, substance abusers, in general, tend to be fragile, lonely individuals who develop rigid adaptive defenses (Wallace, 1978). It is this combination of vulnerability, social isolation and rigid adaptive defenses that is best treated through a group process; a process that utilizes the capacity of a group for both confrontation and support.

TREATMENT FOCUS WITH SUBSTANCE ABUSERS

Although substance abusers come to treatment with a variety of problems, it is important that clinicians utilize what Marsha Vannicelli (1989) calls the "hierarchical treatment" approach, i.e., that the problem of highest crisis potential is treated first. For substance abusers, the problem of highest crisis potential is their abuse of alcohol and other drugs.

Moreover, during early recovery, substance abusers–in particular those dependent on central nervous system depressants such as alcohol, barbiturates and phenothiazines such as Valium–suffer from temporary cognitive impairment, i.e., their abstract reasoning, and their ability to think flexibly and to learn new information, are impaired. Consequently, many substance abusers are often physiologically incapable of psychological changes resulting from insight and cognitive realignment until approximately 12 to 18 months following cessation of substance use.

Therefore, during the early phase of group treatment, a phase that often is prolonged with substance abusers compared to other populations, the group process should focus on the development of group cohesion, introjection of group norms and the establishment of trust in an authority figure. At the same time, the leader needs to help group members see and understand the relationship between substance abuse and the present difficulties in their lives, and encourage the members to explore alternative ways of coping.

While some degree of anxiety and conflict are generally important components of motivation and change (Harticollis & Harticollis, 1980), conflict and anxiety may be counterproductive when dealing with substance abusing clients on an out-patient basis. Therefore, during the early phases of group development, levels of anxiety and conflict should be minimized through extensive use of structure and repetition. The typical defensive features of substance abusing group members, or what Wallace (1978) calls the preferred defense system, consisting of such defenses as denial, rationalization, projection, intellectualization and minimization, should be redirected and built upon, not challenged. The narcissism and grandiosity of the substance abuser can be refocused toward helping other group members instead of being confronted directly and thus leading to power struggles and narcissistic wounds.

Although group members may touch on such important issues as self-image, family and peer relations, financial and legal problems, sexual activities and dysfunctions, health concerns, fears of success and failure, difficulties with self-assertion and appropriate expressions of anger, during the early phase of group treatment members should not be encouraged to look at themselves beyond a rather shallow and superficial level. Only gradually should the focus be shifted from such a supportive model to a here-and-now, interactional group model a la Yalom (Yalom, Block, Bond, Zimmerman & Qualls, 1978; Yalom, 1985) geared toward personality or characterological changes.

A MODEL OF GROUP TREATMENT

The author has found it helpful to conceptualize the early phases of group treatment with substance abusing clients by utilizing Otto

Kernberg's model of supportive therapy which he developed for use with borderline patients (Kernberg 1975, 1986). While not all substance abusers are borderline, many exhibit borderline characteristics during their drug or alcohol use and in early recovery (Goldstein, 1993). Consequently Kernsberg's model offers a basic treatment framework that can be modified as needed.

The author's modification and application of this model to group treatment of substance abusing clients is provided below. The components of this tripartite model consist of: environmental intervention, clarification and confrontation, and support.

Environmental Intervention

The focus of environmental intervention is on curtailing the acting out behaviors and decreasing anxiety by establishing a predictable structure and setting limits both inside and outside the group.

As 12-step groups such as Alcoholics Anonymous (AA) or Narcotics Anonymous (NA) have found, despite changing group membership and varied content and leadership, the ritualistic format of the group meetings provides safety and security, or what can be termed as a holding environment, " . . . an environment that is safe and nurturing and that set(s) and hold(s) the stage for psychological explorations and development" (Spiegel, 1993:158). Thus, it is crucial that during early phases of group treatment, the leader establishes a predictable structure by holding group meetings at a regular time and place with a more or less consistent and predictable group format and leadership style. The leader has to be much more directive than in traditional insight-oriented therapy, while being careful not to take over the group (Galanter, Castaneda & Franco, 1991).

One of the best ways of establishing structure and setting limits is through clear contracting with group members (Blume, 1978; Yalom, 1985). Contracting with substance abusing clients has to address the following issues:

a. Confidentiality and its limitations
b. Lateness and absences
c. Attending group while under the influence of drug and alcohol
d. Relapses

e. Financial obligations
f. Out-of-group socializing
g. Physical and sexual acting out behaviors, and
h. Concurrent attendance at 12-step meetings

While confidentiality is a cornerstone of all group therapy, with substance abusers, the issue of confidentiality is both more crucial and more complicated. As pointed out by Flores (1988), many substance abusers have engaged in embarrassing and humiliating and even illegal behaviors. Moreover, most possess extremely intropunitive superegos resulting in tremendous feelings of shame. Consequently, the need to reassure group members that their revealing of past illegal and embarrassing behaviors as well as current uncomfortable feelings and thoughts will be kept within the group setting is imperative. Group members must agree not to reveal group membership or group content outside the group. Any breach of confidentiality must be addressed immediately and directly.

On the other hand, the protection of confidentiality on the part of the group leader is less clear cut. The leader must advise the group members of the limitations of confidentiality when homicidal, suicidal and, in many communities, child abuse, material is revealed by a group member. Moreover, the leader has to address the nature of information that he or she will share with referring institutions such as the court system, employers, social agencies and even family members who may contact the therapist both to provide as well as obtain information. In most cases, group members referred by coercive institutions are asked to sign a release allowing the group therapist to provide information regarding the group member's attendance and a general sense of therapeutic progress, without revealing any specific information regarding the content addressed in treatment.

In regard to contact by family members, group members' confidentiality also should be protected. If necessary, referrals for couple or family therapy may be indicated and the author has found couple, multicouple, or multifamily group treatment extremely valuable during later stages of recovery. Finally, the use of drug testing and how and with whom such results are shared also needs to be spelled out during the contracting process.

After the issue of confidentiality is addressed, the question of lateness and absences needs to be negotiated. As a rule, substance abusers tend to be irresponsible when drinking and drugging. Consequently, an essential component of the recovery process includes the establishment of norms regarding assumption of responsibility of group members to arrive on time and attend meetings on a regular basis and to be punctual in paying bills. If for some reason a member is unable to attend a group, he or she needs to notify the group leader prior to the meeting. The leader of a group of substance abusing members, unlike leaders of other kinds of groups, may need to reach out to absent members. Thus, during the contracting phase, group members may be informed that absences will be seen as a cry for help. Absent group members will be contacted immediately after the group by either the group leader or by a previously designated group member who should be chosen by the group on a rotating basis.

Some group therapists ask group members to contract for an initial commitment of twelve sessions in order to allow for the development of group cohesion (Vannicelli, 1982; 1992). Such a commitment, reminiscent of AA suggestion of 90 meetings in 90 days, is highly recommended.

In some groups, members are discouraged from coming into a group if they are late more than ten minutes, while other groups are more tolerant of latecomers. While a group should have the option of negotiating what arrangements are most acceptable to its members, the leader should inform the group that those with excessive lateness and/or absences will be viewed as needing more intensive treatment and as probably not appropriate for an ongoing outpatient group. Acting out behavior, such as absences and lateness, often can be addressed and worked through in the group. However, due to previously discussed dynamics, during the early phases of group treatment, substance abusing clients need the leader's help in establishing and maintaining clear limits.

Financial management is also an important aspect of recovery and needs to be included as part of the contracting process. Since substance abusers usually have been able to find money to obtain drugs or alcohol, it is clinically important that each group member be asked to pay for their treatment even if such payment consists of a token amount.

Attending group while under the influence of a chemical as well as having group members who indicate that they are unable to maintain their alcohol- and drug-free existence in between group sessions is a common occurrence when dealing with substance abusing groups. Group leaders need to offer clear-cut guidelines as to how such situations will be handled even before they arise. In general, it is recommended that group members be informed that intoxicated individuals will be asked to leave the group and return the following week, while those who experience relapses will be asked to explore their inability to maintain their recovery. Members should be told that if a group member is unable to maintain sobriety for more than three successive weeks he or she will be referred to more intensive treatment since they obviously need more help than the group can provide.

While concurrent attendance at 12-step meetings should not be mandated, it is the author's strong belief that such participation aids in the recovery process and should be encouraged by the group leader. Group members should be informed that they are welcome to bring into the group any feelings, both positive and negative, that they experience during their 12-step meetings. However, group leaders should clarify the differences between a self-help group meeting and a professionally run group therapy (Cooper, 1987; Galanter et al., 1991; Spiegel, 1993).

The final aspects of contracting should address the issues of out-of-group socializing as well as physical and sexual acting out. Many substance abusers, in particular those abusing central nervous system stimulants such as cocaine and amphetamines, as well as alcohol abusers, have a history of sexual acting out and some have difficulties with proper sexual expression during the recovery process. It is therefore therapeutic for group members to contract not to engage in sexual relations with other group members while being encouraged to verbally express their positive feelings toward one another. The same applies toward expression of anger and other negative feelings, with group members contracting to express such feelings toward other members as well as the group leader verbally rather than physically.

Group members need also to contract that any out-of-group contact among members will be shareable within the group, i.e., that any meeting between group members outside the group, for example, two or more group members meeting each other at an AA group, should be discussed during the next group meeting. It is important for members to realize that both sexual contact as well as out-of-group socializing may lead to formation of subgroups that may interfere with the proper and therapeutic functioning of the group as a whole (Yalom, 1985).

Due to previously mentioned cognitive impairments as well as the tendency to act out, it is best that group members be given a written contract. Such a written contract also serves as a transitional object between the group and the outside world. The written contract, in a brief outline form, can be provided during the first group meeting in the case of a formation of a new group, and ritualized as part of the initiation and contracting as new members come into the group. In either case, such a contract has to be discussed with the whole group in order to allow each group member the opportunity to both challenge and accept, even if superficially, the contract.

Violations of contract enable the group leader to understand the various resistances, character traits and transferences that take place in the group and the resulting discussions become part of the working through process for group members (Flores, 1988; Yalom, 1985).

Clarification and Confrontation

Clarification and confrontation consist of pointing out and explaining the contradictions in behavior between what a person says and does. When dealing with substance abusers, it is very important that any clarification and confrontation be offered in an empathic manner that does not lead to further narcissistic injuries.

Confrontation, whether by the group leader or other group members, should be limited to drinking and drug related behaviors, while soothing, empathic reactions are provided in relation to other feelings and behaviors. The view of substance abuse as a disease is invaluable in helping group members alleviate their feelings of guilt without absolving them from responsibility for future behavior (Straussner, 1993).

Through the modeling of confrontative, yet empathic responses, the leader helps group members connect cause-and-effect behavior thereby developing members' reality testing and judgment. At the same time, group members' introjections of the leader's empathic reactions results in an increase in their self-nurturing and self-soothing feelings. Group members' use of empathic responses with each other further improves object relations.

Support

According to Kernberg (1986), support has two components: affective and cognitive. This author would add a third component: behavioral.

As indicated previously, substance abusers are frequently unable to identify and find expression for their feelings, a condition labelled alexithymia. Therefore, a crucial aspect of affective, or emotional, support is to help group members to identify and express a full range of emotions. The author has found it helpful during a very early group session to distribute a handout with a list of various feelings and ask the members to either identify any of the emotions that they may have experienced during a recent time frame, e.g., last week, or yesterday, or toward the end of a given session, to identify any feelings experienced during that session. The building of such emotional vocabulary is an important aspect of empowering group members and diminishing acting out behavior.

At times, it may be helpful to use such techniques as psychodrama (Buchbinder, 1986) to illuminate emotions and unresolved feeling states. Since, as indicated earlier, the leader needs to maintain a general consistency in approach when working with substance abusing clients, it may be best to integrate such techniques as the empty chair or the use of a double within a regular group treatment session as opposed to conducting a full psychodrama session instead of a typical group meeting.

Cognitive or intellectual support further helps group members to understand, and hopefully change, their behavior. While a therapy group is not an appropriate forum for didactic lecturing by the group leader, it is appropriate for a leader and group members to clarify misinformation, to explore accepted myths and irrational attitudes, and to examine values and priorities. Brief explanations followed by discussions of such topics as how a group works, the progressive nature of addiction, and signs and symptoms of relapse, as well as recommendations of appropriate literature (bibliotherapy) and audio or video materials, particularly on such issues as shame, sexuality and impact of substance abuse on the family, are important components of cognitive support.

For many substance abusing clients, change in behavior often precedes insight. Therefore, group therapy can be used to help members learn such behavioral approaches as communication and problem solving skills, stress management techniques (Brody, 1982) and assertiveness training. The latter is of particular importance to substance abusing women (Straussner, 1985).

ROLE OF LEADER

As indicated earlier, the leader of a group of substance abusers, in particular during the early group phases, has to be more active than in other types of groups: "A passive therapist will be viewed as another bad object who is withholding, dull and lifeless. Addicts are searching for an idealized other who is a model or representation of what they wish they could be" (Flores, 1988: p. 408). The leader needs to help the group members replace their dependency on substances with dependency on the group; to tolerate and cope with disagreement, especially with authority; to learn how to communicate feelings and desires; and help the group deal with acting out and resistant behaviors.

A common dilemma for therapists dealing with substance abusing clients is the issue of self disclosure, or what Yalom (1985) refers to as the transparency of the therapist. It is not unusual for group members to enquire whether the leader is him/herself recovering from substance abuse. A leader of a short term, time-limited group (e.g., 12 sessions or less) may find it therapeutic to briefly, and non-defensively, state his/her own status in regard to alcohol and drug use and abuse, keeping in mind that a current user of illegal drugs, even such "soft" drugs as marijuana, should not be leading a group whose members are struggling with recovery from drugs and alcohol (Flores, 1988). On the other hand, the leader of a long term group may find it more helpful to use the approach recommended by Vannicelli (1989) whose policy is to tell patients asking any personal questions the following statement: "Generally, I do not find it useful to share personal information about myself. However, I'd be interested in knowing more about how this particular question might be important to you, and how a given answer of one sort or another might be useful" (p. 121). Such statement allows for further clarification of the intent of the questioner without closing off discussion.

The final, but critical, issue for the leader is that of countertransference. Winnicott's (1949) separation of objective countertransference, i.e., the reaction of the therapist to the feelings induced by a patient's dynamics and behaviors, and subjective countertransference, i.e., the therapist's reactions to a patient based on the therapist's own dynamics, are helpful concepts when dealing with substance abusing clients.

The provocative, acting-out and self-destructive, as well as needy attitudes and behaviors of many substance abusing clients often trigger unconscious negative or otherwise unhelpful counter-reactions (Levinson & Straussner, 1978) on the part of many group leaders. Such reactions need to be understood and addressed in a therapeutic manner instead of having the therapist act out the patient's induced feelings. The same needs to be said when the therapist reacts to a group member based on his/her subjective countertransferential reaction, an area of special concern when the therapist has unresolved issues regarding his/her own or familial substance abuse (Straussner, 1993).

CONCLUSION

As pointed out by Flores (1988), rather than view a substance abuser as someone who does not want to stop using alcohol or other drugs, it may be better to conceptualize such individual as someone who does not realize the possibility of an alternate lifestyle. It is through the therapeutic use of groups for alcohol and other drug abusing individuals and through the power of the group process that such alternate lifestyles can be best exemplified.

The power of groups, for both good and bad, has long been recognized in literary, philosophical and therapeutic writings. The use of group therapy for substance abusing individuals can thus be viewed as both the best and the most difficult treatment approach, with the early phases of the group process playing a particularly important role in maintaining alcohol and other drug abusing individuals in group treatment. Such treatment calls for a sensitive, caring and self-aware group leader with specialized knowledge and skills in both addictions and group dynamics.

REFERENCES

Blume, S. B. (1985). Group psychotherapy in the treatment of alcoholism. In S. Zimberg, J. Wallace, & S. Blume (Eds.), *Practical approaches to alcoholism psychotherapy.* New York: Plenum.

Brandler, S. & Roman, C. (1991) *Social work with groups.* New York: The Haworth Press, Inc.

Brody, A. (1982). S.O.B.E.R.: A stress management program for recovering alcoholics. In M. Altman & R. Crocker (Eds.), *Social Groupwork & Alcoholism.* New York: The Haworth Press, Inc.

Buchbinder, J. (1986). Gestalt therapy and its application to alcoholism treatment. *Alcoholism Treatment Quarterly, 13*(2), 49-67.

Cooper, D. E. (1987). The role of group psychotherapy in the treatment of substance abusers. *American Journal of Psychotherapy, 41*(1), 55-67.

Flores, P. J. (1988). *Group psychotherapy with addicted populations.* New York: The Haworth Press, Inc.

Galanter, M., Castaneda, R., & Franco, H. (1991). Group therapy and self-help groups. In R. J. Frances & S. I. Miller (Eds.) *Clinical textbook of addictive disorders.* New York: Guilford Press.

Goldstein, E. G. (1993). The borderline substance abuser. In S.L.A. Straussner (Ed.), *Clinical work with substance-abusing clients.* New York: Guilford Press.

Harticollis, P. & Harticollis, P. C. (1980). Alcoholism, borderline and narcissistic disorders: A psychoanalytic overview. In W. Fann, I. Karacan, A. Porkory & R. S. Williams (Eds.), *Phenomenology and treatment of alcoholism.* New York: Spectrum.

Kernberg, O. F. (1975). *Borderline conditions and Pathological Narcissism.* New York: Jason Aronson.

Kernberg, O. F. (1986). *Severe personality disorders.* New Haven, CT: Yale University Press.

Khantzian, E. J., Halliday, K. S. & McAuliffe, W. E. (1990) *Addiction and the vulnerable self: Modified dynamic group therapy for substance abusers.* New York: Guilford Press.

Levinson, V. & Straussner, S. L. A. (1978). Social Workers as 'enablers' in the treatment of alcoholics. *Social Casework, 59*(1), 14-20.

Spiegel, B. R. (1993). 12-Step programs as a treatment modality. In S. L. A. Straussner (Ed.), *Clinical work with substance-abusing clients.* New York: Guilford Press.

Straussner, S. L. A. (1993). Assessment and treatment of clients with alcohol and other drug abuse problems: An overview. In S. L. A. Straussner (Ed.), *Clinical work with substance-abusing clients.* New York: Guilford Press.

Straussner, S. L. A. (1985). Alcoholism in women: Current knowledge and implications for treatment. In D. Cook, S. L. A. Straussner & C. Fewell (Eds.), *Psychosocial issues in the treatment of alcoholism.* New York: The Haworth Press, Inc.

Vannicelli, M. (1982). Group psychotherapy with alcoholics: Special techniques. *Journal of Studies on Alcohol, 43,* 17-37.

Vannicelli, M. (1989). *Group psychotherapy with adult children of alcoholics: Treatment techniques and countertransference considerations.* New York: The Guilford Press.

Vannicelli, M. (1992). *Removing the roadblocks: Group psychotherapy with substance abusers and family members.* New York: The Guilford Press.

Wallace, J. (1978). Working with the preferred defense structure of the recovering alcoholic. In S. Zimberg, J. Wallace, & S. Blume (Eds.), *Practical approaches to alcoholism psychotherapy.* New York: Plenum.

Winnicott, D. W. (1949). Hate in the countertransference. *The International Journal of Psycho-Analysis, 30*(2), 69-74.

Yalom, I. D. (1985). *The theory and practice of group psychotherapy.* (3rd ed.). New York: Basic Books.

Yalom, I. D., Block, S., Bond, G., Zimmerman, E. & Qualls, B. (1978). Alcoholics in interactional group therapy. *Archives of General Psychiatry, 35,* 419-425.

Outpatient Group Psychotherapy with Chemically Dependent and Cluster-B Personality Disordered Male Clients

Darrell C. Greene, PhD
L. Donald McVinney, MSSW, ACSW, CSW, CAC

SUMMARY. This article discusses dynamics and interventions specific to group work with chemically dependent and personality disordered men in outpatient treatment. A model of group treatment is presented that combines interpersonal approaches with cognitive-behavioral strategies. The article highlights group issues of limit setting, interpersonal distortions, and aggression as well as the challenges and rewards of providing group services to this population. *[Article copies available for a fee from The Haworth Document Delivery Service: 1-800-342-9678. E-mail address: getinfo@haworth.com]*

INTRODUCTION

While there are extensive references in the literature on personality disorders, chemical dependency, and increasingly, dual disor-

---

Darrell C. Greene is in private practice in New York City. He specializes in chemical dependency issues. L. Donald McVinney is Director of Triangle Treatment at the Robinson Institute, New York City.

Address correspondence to: L. Donald McVinney, Columbia University School of Social Work, McVickar Hall, 622 West 113th Street, New York, NY 10025.

[Haworth co-indexing entry note]: "Outpatient Group Psychotherapy with Chemically Dependent and Cluster-B Personality Disordered Male Clients." Greene, Darrell C. and L. Donald McVinney. Co-published simultaneously in *Journal of Chemical Dependency Treatment* (The Haworth Press, Inc.) Vol. 7, No. 1/2, 1997, pp. 81-96; and: *Chemical Dependency Treatment: Innovative Group Approaches* (ed: L. Donald McVinney) The Haworth Press, Inc., 1997, pp. 81-96. Single or multiple copies of this article are available for a fee from The Haworth Document Delivery Service [1-800-342-9678, 9:00 a.m. - 5:00 p.m. (EST). E-mail address: getinfo@haworth.com].

81

ders, less information may be available to providers that describes group practice with chemically dependent and personality disordered clients. This lack of information may be explained by the following: (1) the predominance of individually-oriented psychoanalytic theorists describing personality disorders, (2) the relatively recent recognition of coexisting psychiatric conditions by providers in the field of chemical dependency, (3) a general antipathy to diagnostic categorization by group practitioners, and (4) recommendations by group practitioners to screen out personality disordered clients from group inclusion because of presumed "inappropriateness." While these factors may create a vacuum of descriptive material on chemically dependent and personality disordered clients and their treatment in groups, the group therapist engaged in the provision of services to addicted populations is well aware of their presence, complexity, and need for care.

This article will discuss theory, define interpersonal themes, and present intervention strategies specific to group work in an outpatient setting with the largest segment of the personality disordered and chemically dependent client: the Cluster-B, or "Dramatic" subtype (Drake and Valliant, 1985; Helzer and Pryzbeck, 1988; Hesselbrock, Meyer and Keener, 1985; Khantzian and Treece, 1985; Koenigsberg, Kaplan, Gilmore and Cooper, 1985; Johnson and Connelley, 1981; Nace, Saxon and Shore, 1983; Rounsaville, Eyre, Weissman and Kleber, 1983). It is hoped that this article will offer the group leader practical guidance when assisting perhaps one's most challenging male clients: those who present with both chemical dependency and Borderline, Narcissistic, Histrionic, or Antisocial Personality Disorders (American Psychiatric Association, 1994).

Theories of Relationship Between Personality Disorders and Chemical Dependency

Whether conceptualized through models of conflict (Wurmser, 1987), ego psychology (Wallace, 1994), self psychology (Khantzian, 1981), or object relations (Krystal, 1994), psychoanalytic theory suggests chemical dependency and personality disorders are intimately entwined. Forrest (1983), for example, states alcoholism "is a product of intense and profound narcissistic need and entitlement deprivation . . . The alcoholic is characterologically and behaviorally similar to the character behavior disorder or sociopath" (pp. 17-18). Kohut (1977, pp. vii-ix) writes " . . . the addict, finally, craves the drug because the drug seems to him to be capable of curing the central defect in his self. It becomes for him the substitute for the self-object which failed him traumatically at a time when he should still have had the feeling of omnipotently controlling its responses in accordance with his needs as if it were a part of himself." Similarly, Levin (1987, p. 378) states, "It is abysmally low self-esteem, doubts about being real or of existing at all, and terror of fragmentation that addicts, including alcohol addicts, try to remediate by their addictions." Finally, Hartocollis and Hartocollis (1994, p. 219) conclude, "On evidence from current psychoanalytic reports and our own research, we propose that alcoholic patients are Borderline, Narcissistic or both."

In contrast to accounts of personality disorders promoting the symptom of addiction, Schuckit (1973) suggests two alternative potential relationships between variables:

1. Character pathology is a consequence of dependency.
2. Commonly shared factors lead to both addiction and personality disorder.

Valliant (1983, p. 235), supporting the first relationship, reports in his longitudinal study of alcoholics that "in pre-morbid personality, the majority of alcoholics may be no different from non-alcoholics." Bean-Bayog (1986) emphasizes the trauma of addiction, rather than early childhood development, in explaining personality features of chemically dependent clients. Nace (1987) highlights the impact of psychoactive substances on character, suggesting that features of impulsivity, decreased frustration tolerance, self-centeredness, grandiosity, and affect intolerance are consequences of chronic substance use rather than expressions of underlying personality pathology.

Others suggest the existence of primary factors influencing both personality disturbances and addictions. Sher and Trull (1994), for example, have found that Antisocial Personality Disordered and substance abusing clients may share an underlying drive for risk-taking. In addition, evidence is available supporting contentions that Conduct and later Antisocial Disorders and drug abuse may be symptoms of Attention Deficit Hyperactive Disorder, or ADHD (Mannuzza, Klein, Bessler, Malloy, and La Padula, 1993), and that cocaine abuse may reflect attempts at self-medicating attentional deficits in some clients (Nace, 1987).

In summary, it is suggested that various theoretical models that describe the relationship between chemical dependency and personality disorders represent subsamples of clients receiving chemical dependency treatment. Clients for whom personality features mimic personality disorders as an effect of chemical dependency will present within a normal range following a significant period of abstinence, or once treated for underlying Axis I disorders. For others, however, the ongoing treatment of chemical dependency is significantly complicated by personality disorders. Even with prolonged abstinence, clients may reveal severe personality psychopathology. This may be particularly true for involuntary clients or those who have consistently failed in prior attempts to maintain abstinence (Goldstein, 1993). With persistently "problematic" clients in group settings, the likelihood of a concomitant personality disorder is significantly increased (Nace, 1987).

Chemical Dependency, Dramatic Personality Disorders and Treatment Goals

Whether personality psychopathology of the dramatic type is primary, secondary to substance abuse, or a function of a third underlying disorder, the group therapist providing chemical dependency treatment must respond to behavior as immediately presented while maintaining a fundamental focus on the internalization of recovery. Linehan (1987; 1992) offers the following steps to be used in treating clients with personality disorders and substance abuse:

1. Interrupt and address suicidal or self-injurious behavior.
2. Deal with behavior jeopardizing therapeutic involvement.
3. Treat serious and disruptive conditions, such as substance abuse.
4. With successful control of chemical dependency, attend to problems in living, and
5. Address client life goals and self-actualization.

In contrast to Linehan's treatment hierarchy, it is suggested that as chemical use represents self-injurious behavior and jeopardizes treatment, it must be prioritized with addicted and personality-disordered clients. Adapting Linehan's model, it is recommended that appropriate treatment of chemically dependent and personality disordered clients requires attending to multiple crises while prioritizing recovery as essential to the interruption of self- and interpersonally-destructive behavior.

Recovery in chemically dependent and personality disordered male clients is facilitated by the interruption of maladaptive behaviors and schemata, and by their replacement with strategies both sustaining abstinence and promoting alternative forms of gratification. Therefore, the initial goals of treatment include (1) creating a therapeutic alliance, (2) recommending the development of a recovery support network by encouraging involvement in 12-Step programs and the acquisition of a sponsor, (3) introducing relapse prevention, (4) discouraging continued contact with peers who continue to use psychoactive substances, (5) teaching the importance of avoiding relapse "triggers" that stimulate thoughts of drug-taking, and (6) teaching methods to interrupt cravings (Washton and Stone-Washton, 1990). Intermediate goals include assisting clients in (1) developing skills to acquire and maintain social contact and support, (2) increasing awareness of behaviors, communications, and constructs that distance or alienate others, (3) identifying and participating in leisure activities that do not involve alcohol or other drug use, (4) recognizing and labeling emotions, and (5) discovering the interplay among feelings, cravings, and actions, and learning to tolerate unpleasant feelings.

Once abstinence is achieved and solidified, longer term treatment of chemically dependent and Cluster-B Personality Disordered clients is possible. Long-term goals involve the deconstruction of underlying distortions of self and others through an analysis of here-and-now transactions, as well as through historic review and reparation of past traumatizations. This latter process must be undertaken cautiously with all chemically dependent clients, but particularly so with clients who have co-existing personality disorders so as not to jeopardize abstinence and evoke psychological crisis.

Group Work with Chemically Dependent
and B-Cluster Personality Disordered Clients

There are numerous advantages to group work with personality disordered and chemically dependent clients. In a more direct and effective manner than individual psychotherapy, groups may address client egocentrism, anxiety, despair, withdrawal, anger, feelings of boundary diffusion and dependency, inappropriate conduct, and social skill development (Horwitz, 1987; Macaskill, 1980; 1982). A group modality offers clients multiple relationships with group members with whom they may form attachments, discover interpersonal dynamics, and learn to identify. In addition, client-therapist transference and countertransference may be tempered and made more manageable within the context of a group. The latter may be particularly useful with Cluster-B and chemically dependent clients whose impaired regulation of affect and low tolerance for closeness may make individual therapy particularly threatening.

While groups offer these advantages, it is also important to recognize challenges to the group leader in sustaining an atmosphere of safety, interrupting destructive hostilities, instilling and maintaining hope, and applying interventions according to group development and individual client capacity. These features are crucial to any group treatment but they are especially so in the treatment of clients with co-existing diagnoses of chemical dependency and Cluster-B Personality Disorders.

Group Approach

It is the authors' experience that the following model of group treatment has been particularly effective in an outpatient setting with Dramatic Personality Disordered and chemically dependent male clients. This model incorporates interpersonal approaches to group psychotherapy with cognitive-behavioral strategies. It differs from traditional interpersonal treatment by (1) adopting an initially directive therapeutic style with clearly defined limits and norms, (2) introducing psychoeducational material on addictions, relapse prevention, and recovery, and (3) by incrementally advancing a more exploratory and open-ended approach once sobriety and group cohesion have developed. A general overview of theory is presented here as are group dynamics and therapeutic intervention strategies specific to group work with chemically dependent and personality disordered male clients.

Limits and Norms

Structuring the boundaries of the group and establishing behavioral limits for group members are essential to effective group treatment with personality disordered and chemically dependent male clients. While limit-setting predominantly addresses the "don'ts" of the group, normative behavior is described, modeled, and reinforced by the group leader, and progressively, by group members. At the beginning of each session, group members are asked (1) to sign-in as a record of attendance, and to report the number of 12-Step meetings they have attended since the last group session, (2) indicate their status of engagement with a sponsor, and (3) identify whether they have "slipped" since the last group session. During this sign-in period, members are asked to briefly "check in" with the group by reporting on any issues or conflicts they have experienced between sessions, or to discuss any addiction-specific concerns or successes. This presented material will often organize the content of the session. At the close of each group session, group members are asked to identify something they will remember, contemplate, or internalize from the group experience. These boundary defining interventions (1) allow clients to express concerns immediately, (2) inform the leader as to the client's experience of the group, (3) emphasize the importance of employing the group, (4) implicitly express equal value among all members, (5) set immediate limits on client monopolization, (6) support differences of experience, (7) inform members of the importance of utilizing the group experience between sessions, (8) structure empathic listening and identification, and (9) establish a ritual in order to facilitate consistency and group cohesion.

As the group begins to discuss topics of relapse prevention strategies, actual relapses, identifying triggers, problems in acquiring 12-Step sponsors, emerging conflicts with sponsors, or discomfort at 12-Step meetings, personality features become exposed or erupt, and require immediate intervention by the group leader in order to sustain a "working group."

Interpersonal Group Treatment

According to interpersonal theory, psychological disturbance is a function of disturbed interpersonal relationships, manifested by dysfunctional interactions. Parataxic distortions, or rigid and generalized patterns of communications sustained by memory and symbolization, are transferred onto present exchanges (Sullivan, 1953). These patterns of communication elicit predictable reactions resulting in a re-experiencing of interpersonal expectations. Patterns of exchange thus shape one's processing of information into repeated narratives or schemata about the self and others (Schaefer, 1992). Treatment, therefore, requires the "experiential disconfirmation within the therapeutic relationship of the patient's fundamental maladaptive conceptualizations of the self in relationship to the interpersonal environment and the patient's recognition of his or her related contributions" (Schaefer, 1992, p. 40). Interrupting distortions results in an expansion of choice, a broadening of interpersonal capacities, and a "rewriting" of scripts so that new patterns of relating may be established.

Personality Disorders, Chemical Dependency and Constructions

The belief systems manifested by Dramatic Personality Disordered clients are the filter through which active addiction and recovery from addiction are colored. The authors suggest that while those with personality disorders may use substances for a variety of theoretical and professionally-defined reasons, clients also ascribe meaning to their behavior. The client with Antisocial Personality Disorder, for example, may construe his substance use as an expression of rebellion, the Narcissist as marking his superiority, the Histrionic as fulfilling his need for excitement, and the Borderline as that which soothes without the risk of abandonment. Thus, substance use becomes a projection of a client's view of himself that validates and supports pre-existing schemata and predicts behavioral strategies employed by clients throughout the course of addiction. Decisions to engage in chemical dependency treatment are also based upon experiences that confront or threaten self constructions. Thus, the enrollment in treatment may be preceded by the client with Antisocial Personality Disorder seeing himself as weak, the Narcissist as worthless, the Histrionic as a bore, and the Borderline as completely "bad." Each fears himself slipping into the role of the "Other."

Conflicts with participation in 12-Step fellowship meetings and the acquisition of a sponsor may occur as a consequence of interpersonal difficulties. For example, the client with Antisocial Personality Disorder may believe himself to be a loner who cannot "surrender" to the program and fears or imagines the inevitable "attack" of a sponsor. If a sponsor relationship is initiated, the Antisocial client may have great difficulty maintaining responsible contact, or may attempt to manipulate and deceive the sponsor. Similarly, clients with Narcissistic Personality Disorder may overwhelm their sponsors with a relentless questioning of the 12-Step program and by rigidly maintaining a belief in their personal difference from "other addicts." The Histrionic client may overwhelm his sponsor with "crises." The Borderline client may idealize and then psychologically attack his sponsor in reaction to perceived slights or accusations of unavailability.

Given these beliefs, male clients with co-existing personality disorders and chemical dependency will, in all likelihood, experience great difficulty engaging in 12-Step programs. Thus, providers who simply recommend or require 12-Step program participation without acknowledging the role of personal constructs that problematize client participation may unwittingly "set-up" clients for failure and jeopardize a client's recovery or continuation in treatment. It is essential for the group therapist to anticipate, predict and attempt to proactively resolve complications or conflicts associated with 12-Step programs for chemically dependent and personality disordered clients. When such conflicts do arise, the group leader should attempt to resolve them using the group process rather than blaming clients for the very limitations around which they have sought help.

In keeping with self and other constructs and strategies of self-care, Dramatic Personality Disordered clients may demonstrate tremendous difficulty tolerating the experience of group psychotherapy. Group members may respond to one another in ways that reinforce parataxic distortions. Table 1 suggests potential client behavior, group members' responses, and associated client conclusions that reinforce personal constructs.

Thus, self constructs are maintained through feedback loops requiring therapeutic interruption and analysis if clients are to profit from or even remain in group treatment, increase an awareness of their interpersonal behavior, and fortify their commitment to recovery.

INTERVENTIONS

Anger

The early expression of member-to-member anger in chemical dependency groups with personality disordered clients is predictable, and is often elicited well before the safety of group cohesiveness has been established. The interruption of hostility is essential to the establishment of a group and necessitates active involvement by the leader. Conflict may be reduced through therapeutic triangulation, in which clinicians encourage clients to "talk through the therapist" rather than directly to one another. Goals

TABLE 1.

Client Behavior	Member Response	Client Conclusion
1. Disregard for norms (Antisocial)	Exploited, angry	"Safer alone"
2. Haughty, self-centered (Narcissistic)	Indifferent, angry	"Rejected"
3. Excitable (Histrionic)	Stimulated, then unresponsive, bored	"Uncared for"
4. Demanding (Borderline)	Avoidance, angry	"Alone again"

for the group facilitator attempting to monitor client anger include tracking behaviors that evoke reactions of anger, teaching communication styles to group members that offer specific and behavioral feedback rather than derogatory labels, assisting group members in distinguishing between intent versus the effect of communications (i.e., content vs. tone) and assisting members in apprehending transferential reactions, or why only certain behaviors seem to evoke so strong a reprisal. Conflicts between members are reframed as gifts in offering participants opportunities to gain greater self-awareness and in allowing for practice in conflict resolution.

Anger towards the therapist can also be particularly intense with personality disordered and chemically dependent clients, and can be employed as an attempt to challenge authority, ventilate rage, obtain attention, communicate jealousy, or assert failures in provider empathy. While rebellion against the leader may be a healthy dynamic in typical group formation by equalizing power (Levine, 1979), "annihilation" of the group leader may extinguish any potential for cohesion in groups with addicted and personality disordered clients (Walker, 1992).

Clients require control and limit setting when they are angered as much as a continuation of warmth and involvement (Kernberg, 1984; Kohut, 1971). If both are presented, it is suggested that the group therapist will neither be construed as a pushover nor a perpetrator, but rather as someone capable of tolerating and containing client rage. As Higgit and Foragy (1992, p. 30) suggest, "the therapist must not retaliate against or abandon the patient with his rage, nor should the therapist relinquish therapeutic responsibility and feign indifference to slights and threats."

Group Cohesion

Many clients with chemical dependency and personality disorders have great difficulty joining groups. Groups may be experienced as producing an overwhelming flood of anxiety. As Pines (1978) notes, Borderline clients are particularly susceptible to a pathological and overwhelming identification with all members, inducing profound confusion and excitement. Alternatively, Antisocial personalities may experience the group as a threat to their independence. Client demands for attention, expectations of admiration, and limited empathy may all conspire to make integration into a group problematic. Interventions aimed at increasing awareness, interrupting dysfunctional patterns of relating, and promoting safety are crucial to successful inclusion. For many, this may require both group and individual psychotherapy in order to process a client's experience, sustain levels of alliance, facilitate coping strategies, and promote understanding of interpersonal dynamics (Wory, 1980).

Dependency/Counterdependency

The evolution of group process may be restricted by chemically dependent and personality disordered clients' expressions of dependency and counterdependency. Members may employ the therapist as the only object in the group capable of offering approval, acceptance, nurturance, and help. As Yalom (1975, p. 234) comments: "Patients appear to behave as if salvation emanates solely or primarily from the therapist, if only they can discover what he wants them to do." Interventions require directing clients' attentions to fellow group members, encouraging member-to-member communication and feedback, and reinforcing the value of group support.

Counterdependent maneuvers may also interfere with group process. The help requesting-then-rejecting complainer may attempt to manage feelings of helplessness by defeating caregivers in what has been described as a game of "Why Don't You–Yes, But" (Berne, 1961). Interruption of the game requires assisting the group in making it transparent and offering alternative modes of relating. The difficulties of counterdependent clients in accepting care, however, are often ongoing and will require sustained interventions countering self and other constructions until a client may find supportiveness palatable.

Expanding Schemata and Strategies

Beck and Freeman (1990, p. 42) describe the overdeveloped and underdeveloped strategies of personality disordered clients. Table 2 illustrates these ideas.

TABLE 2.

Personality Disorder	Overdeveloped Strategy	Underdeveloped Strategy
Narcissistic	Self-aggrandizement Competitiveness	Sharing Group Identification
Antisocial	Combativeness Exploitiveness Predation	Empathy Reciprocity Social Sensitivity
Histrionic	Exhibitionism Expressiveness Impressionism	Reflectiveness Control Systemization
Borderline	Dichotomous Thinking Aggression Chameleon	Continuity Impulse Control Identity

These strategic generalizations are readily apparent in the chemically dependent personality disordered client. The following techniques are recommended to enlarge client strategies and to problematize overemployed modes of relating:

1. Guided discovery, facilitating the recognition of stereotypical patterns of interpretation.
2. Questioning or labeling inaccurate inferences in order to increase awareness of bias and automatic thought patterns.
3. Examining explanations for other's behavior, and
4. Scaling, or translating extreme interpretations into dimensional terms, thus interrupting dichotomous thinking.

Other techniques that deconstruct overgeneralized patterns and reinforce new strategies include direct instruction in underemployed interpersonal patterns, and enlarging empathy through historic review and group support.

CONCLUSIONS

While far from definitive, this article has presented a model of treatment with chemically dependent male clients with co-existing

Personality Disorders. The authors have outlined group themes that emerge and group interventions that have been found to be effective with this population. It in no way purports to be a formula for global success nor does it begin to describe the tremendous challenges experienced by providers working with this population. However, it may offer the practitioner concrete guidance in formulating treatment strategies with chemically dependent and personality disordered clients. While there is a common misperception that clients with addictions and personality disorders, because of interpersonal deficits, are unsuited to the group modality, it has been the authors' experience that group work can greatly benefit clients with Antisocial, Borderline, Histrionic, and Narcissistic Personality Disorders and effectively treat their chemical dependency in a way that individual psychotherapy alone can, at best, only approximate, and at worst, dangerously prolong.

REFERENCES

American Psychiatric Association. (1994). *Diagnostic Criteria from DSM-IV.* Washington, DC: American Psychiatric Association.

Bean-Bayog, M. (1986). Psychopathology produced by alcoholism. In R.E. Myer (Ed.) *Psychopathology and addictive disorders.* (334-335). New York: Guilford Press.

Beck, A.T. & Freeman, A. (1990). *Cognitive therapy of personality disorders.* New York: Guilford Press.

Berne, E. (1961). *Transactional analysis in psychotherapy.* New York: Robi Press.

Drake, R.E. & Vaillant, G.E. (1985). A validity study of Axis II of DSM-III. *American Journal of Psychiatry, 42,* 353-558.

Forrest, G.G. (1983). *Alcoholism, narcissism and psychopathology.* New Jersey: Jason Aronson, Inc.

Goldstein, E.G. (1993). The borderline substance abuser. In S.L.A. Staussner (Ed.), *Clinical work with substance-abusing clients* (270-290). New York: Guilford Press.

Hartocollis, P. & Hartocollis, P.C. (1994). Alcoholism, borderline, and narcissistic disorders. In J.D. Levin & R.H. Weiss (Eds.), *The dynamics and treatment of alcoholism* (207-221). New Jersey: Jason Aronson, Inc.

Helzer, J.E. & Pryzbeck, T.R. (1988). The co-occurrence of alcoholism with other psychiatric disorders in the general population and its impact on treatment. *Journal of Studies on Alcohol, 49,* 219-224.

Hesselbrock, M.N., Meyer, R.E. & Keener, J.J. (1985). Psychopathology in hospitalized alcoholics. *Archives of General Psychiatry, 42,* 1050-1055.

Higgit, A. & Foragy, P. (1992). Psychotherapy in borderline and narcissistic personality disorder. *British Journal of Psychiatry, 161,* 23-43.

Horwitz, L. (1987). Indications for group psychotherapy with borderline and narcissistic patients. *Bulletin of the Menninger Clinic, 51,* 248-260.

Johnson, R.P. & Connelly, J.C. (1981). Addicted physicians take a closer look. *Journal of the American Medical Association, 245,* 253-257.

Kernberg, O. (1984). *Seven personality disorders: Psycho-therapeutic strategies.* New Haven, CT: Yale University Press.

Khantzian, E.J. & Treece, C. (1985). DSM-III psychiatric diagnosis of narcotic addicts. *Archives of General Psychology, 42,* 1067-1071.

Khantzian, E.J. (1981). Some treatment implications of ego and self-disturbances in alcoholism. In M.H. Bean and N.E. Zinberg (Eds.), *Dynamic approaches to the understanding and treatment of alcoholism* (163-188). New York: Free Press.

Koenigsberg, H.W., Kaplan, R.D., Gilmore, M.M. & Lopez, A. M. (1985). The relationship between syndrome and personality disorder in DSM-III: Experience with 2,462 patients. *American Journal of Psychiatry, 142,* 207-212.

Kohut, H. (1977). *The restoration of the self.* New York: International University Press.

Krystal, H. (1994). Self- and object-representation in alcoholism and other drug-dependence: Implications for therapy. In J.D. Levin & R.H. Weiss (Eds.), *The dynamics and treatment of alcoholism* (300-310). Northvale, NJ: Jason Aronson, Inc.

Levin, J.D. (1987). *Treatment of alcoholism and other addictions.* Northvale, NJ: Jason Aronson, Inc.

Levine, B. (1979). *Group psychotherapy.* Prospect Heights, IL: Waveland Press, Inc.

Linehan, M.M. (1987). Dialectical behavior therapy in borderline patients. *Bulletin of the Menninger Clinic, 51,* 261-276.

Linehan, M.M. (1992). Behavior therapy, dialectics, and the treatment of borderline personality disorder. In I.D. Silver & M. Rosenbluth (Eds.), *Handbook of borderline disorders* (415-434). Madison, CT: International University Press.

Macaskill, N.D. (1980). The narcissistic care as a focus in the group therapy of the borderline patient. *British Journal of Medical Psychology, 53,* 137-143.

Macaskill, N.D. (1982). Therapeutic factors in group therapy with borderline patients. *International Journal of Group Psychotherapy, 32,* 61-74.

Mannuzza, S., Klein, R.G., Bessler, A., Malloy, P., & LaPadula, M. (1993). Adult outcome of hyperactive boys. *Archives of General Psychiatry, 50,* 565-576.

Nace, E.P., Jaxon, J.J., & Shore, N. (1983). A comparison of borderline and non-borderline alcoholic patients. *Archives of General Psychiatry, 40,* 54-56.

Nace, E.P. (1987). Substance abuse and personality disorder. In D.F. O'Connell (Ed.), *Managing the dually diagnosed patient* (183-189). New York: The Haworth Press, Inc.

Pines, M. (1978). Group analytic psychotherapy of the borderline patient. *Group Analysis, II,* 115-126.

Rounsaville, B.J., Eyre, S.L., Weissman, M.M. & Kleber, H.P. (1983). The Antisocial opiate addict. *Advances in Alcohol and Substance Abuse, 2,* 29-42.

Schaefer, R. (1992). *Retelling a life.* New York: Basic Books.

Schuckit, M.A. (1985). The clinical implications of primary diagnostic groups among alcoholics. *Archives of General Psychiatry, 42,* 1043-1049.

Sher, K.J. and Trull, T.J. (1994). Personality and disinhibiting psychopathology: Alcoholism and Antisocial personality disorder. *Journal of Abnormal Psychology, 103*(1), 92-102.

Sullivan, H.S. (1953). *The interpersonal theory of psychiatry.* New York: Norton.

Vaillant, G.E. (1983). *The natural history of alcoholism.* Cambridge, MA: Harvard University Press.

Walker, R. (1992). Substance abuse and B-Cluster disorders II: Treatment recommendations. *Journal of Psychoactive Drugs, 24*(3), 233-241.

Wallace, J. (1994). Working with the preferred defense structure of the recovering alcoholic. In J.D. Levin and R.H. Weiss (Eds.), *The dynamics and treatment of alcoholism* (222-231). Northvale, NJ: Jason Aronson, Inc.

Washton, A.M. and Stone-Washton, N. (1990). Abstinence and relapse in outpatient cocaine addicts. *Journal of Psychoactive Drugs, 22*(2), 135-147.

Wory, N. (1980). Combined group and individual treatment of borderline and narcissistic patients: heterogeneous vs. homogeneous groups. *International Journal of Group Psychotherapy, 30,* 389-404.

Wurmser, L. (1987). Flight from conscience: Experience with the psychoanalytic treatment of compulsive drug abusers. *Journal of Substance Abuse Treatment, 4,* 169-179.

Yalom, I. (1975). *The theory and practice of group psychotherapy.* New York: Basic Books.

The Model of Multiple Oppression in Group Psychotherapy with HIV-Infected Injecting Drug Users

Fred Millán, PhD
Noel Elia, CSW

SUMMARY. The Model of Multiple Oppression is used to outline the various oppressed group memberships which impact on the lives of Black and Latino HIV-infected injecting drug users. Descriptions of the important issues for each level of oppression are discussed. Clinical examples are given to describe how the factors manifest and what types of clinical interventions are most effective. *[Article copies available for a fee from The Haworth Document Delivery Service: 1-800-342-9678. E-mail address: getinfo@haworth.com]*

Juan is a 33-year-old HIV+ gay Latino who was routinely physically and emotionally abused, along with his siblings, by their father in Puerto Rico where they lived in squalid condi-

Fred Millán is Associate Professor of Psychology/Chair, Department of Psychology, State University of New York/College at Old Westbury, Old Westbury, NY. Noel Elia is affiliated with Montefiore Medical Center.

This publication was made possible by two Ryan White CARE Act grants: grant number BRH970025-03-1 from the Health Resources Services Administration and grant number OHF-4165 administered by the Medical and Health Research Association of New York City. Its contents are solely the responsibility of the authors and do not necessarily represent the official views of HRSA and MHRA.

[Haworth co-indexing entry note]: "The Model of Multiple Oppression in Group Psychotherapy with HIV-Infected Injecting Drug Users." Millán, Fred and Noel Elia. Co-published simultaneously in *Journal of Chemical Dependency Treatment* (The Haworth Press, Inc.) Vol. 7, No. 1/2, 1997, pp. 97-117; and: *Chemical Dependency Treatment: Innovative Group Approaches* (ed: L. Donald McVinney) The Haworth Press, Inc., 1997, pp. 97-117. Single or multiple copies of this article are available for a fee from The Haworth Document Delivery Service [1-800-342-9678, 9:00 a.m. - 5:00 p.m. (EST). E-mail address: getinfo@haworth.com].

tions. The abuse included beatings, threatened homicide (his father slept with a machete next to his bed) and food and sleep deprivation. Shortly after the family moved to New York when he was about 10 years old, Juan was kidnapped by a man in the neighborhood and held captive in an abandoned building for several months. He was sexually abused by this man who also forced him to use drugs. He also witnessed the hanging death of a young girl while being held there. Juan fantasized that his family was trying desperately to find him during this time but when he finally escaped he discovered that they had moved back to Puerto Rico.

Left to fend for himself, Juan survived with some other street kids in abandoned buildings and in cars, stealing everything from food to electricity. Juan describes feeling loved and wanted by his peers. Soon he developed a heroin habit and became involved in criminal activity to support it. He spent 3 years in jail but he describes "doing time" as relatively easy compared to life with his father.

Juan's family (except for his father) have all moved back to New York within the past 10 years. Two brothers and one sister have since died of AIDS. A younger sister is HIV-infected and two more of Juan's brothers are active drug users. His mother has a cocaine habit. Juan is currently in a methadone maintenance program, where he has been in psychotherapy for two years.

Cherie is a 42-year-old HIV+ African American heterosexual married woman, who was reared by both her working class parents, in a large family of 16 children. Cherie describes her childhood as happy, yet she recalls feeling lonely despite the presence of so many family members. Her parents drank and Cherie explains that her introduction to drugs began with alcohol use. The family still lives in New York and Cherie remains connected to them. She has told them about her HIV status. Cherie's 3 children had been removed from her about 10 years ago due to her drug addiction. They are currently living in kinship foster care with an aunt in Brooklyn. She has not disclosed her HIV+ status to them. Within the past three years two of Cherie's brothers have died from AIDS as have her two closest girlfriends. Her oldest sister died recently from a massive heart attack. Her husband of 2 years is dying of end stage AIDS. Cherie has decided to stay in her own apartment with her husband despite an offer by her mother to move back to Brooklyn.

Group psychotherapy with HIV-infected people of color with histories of injecting drug use presents intricate and complex problems. This population has had to deal with multiple traumas throughout their lives, as well as serious stigmatization due to many of the negative stereotypes attributed to the groups they represent (Elia & Millán, 1994).

This article will present the Model of Multiple Oppression (MMO) (Millán & Elia, 1995) to demonstrate the many layers of oppressed group membership that are simultaneously impinging upon our patients' lives. The previous cases will be used to demonstrate the application of the model.

New York City is currently the U.S. city with the highest number of AIDS cases among its residents, a total of 71,934 (CDC, 1995). Overall, New York City's total is higher than any state other than New York State (of which its total is part) and California (CDC, 1995).

The New York State Department of Health (1995) reports that Blacks account for 40.3% and Latinos account for another 30.7% of the adult AIDS cases in New York City. Both figures are disproportionate to the total number of the two groups in the city.

For blacks, injecting drug users (IDUs) accounted for 53.5% of the male cases and 61% of the female cases. The category of men who had sex with men who were also IDUs (MSWM/IDU) added another 4.7%. So, for the men, injecting drug use was involved in 58.2% of the cases (NYS Department of Health, 1995).

For Latinos, IDU accounted for 57.5% of the males and 60.2% of the female adult cases. Latino MSWM/IDU added another 4.3%, bringing the male injecting drug use-related total to 61.8% (NYS Department of Health, 1995). These figures demonstrate the high correlation between injecting drug use and HIV infection for Blacks and Latinos in New York City.

The MMO arose from the clinical work of the authors with these patients on the AIDS Mental Health Team at three methadone maintenance programs in the Bronx. The patients present a wide variety of issues which are not always directly related to their HIV status. The authors were impressed by the complexity and severity of the patient presentations, as well as by their interrelatedness. For example, oftentimes medical providers felt patients were noncompliant, or in denial about their HIV issues, when in actuality they were focusing on other pressing concerns, or acting out their despair. The model is an attempt to order and understand some of these issues, and their implications, for our patients.

MODEL OF MULTIPLE OPPRESSION: UNDERLYING PRINCIPLES

While the MMO does not purport to be all-inclusive, it does demonstrate some of the most important factors that these injecting drug users related to the authors. The model is a way of looking at the multiply oppressed person with AIDS (MOPWA). While white patients from other socioeconomic brackets may also experience oppression (including dysfunctional families, constricting gender roles, sexual identity issues, substance abuse and HIV), we believe that race and class are uniquely powerful oppressed group memberships which have a devastating impact on the poor patient of color. Minimal survival for the MOPWA therefore becomes profoundly more precarious.

The authors make some fundamental value judgements about these patients which inform the underlying principles of the Model of Multiple Oppression. First, we believe that all human beings are intrinsically worthy. In our model this is demonstrated by the inside of the Self circle (see Figure 1). Second, we believe that our patients are misperceived by society as persons who "can't cope" or who "aren't strong enough" to care for themselves and their families. We find that their apparently "self-destructive" life choices and chaotic existence often make perfect sense when viewed within the context of their psychosocial history. We experience our patients as remarkably courageous and resourceful at negotiating their very survival in a hostile, and often violent life space. Third, we feel that patients are interested in moving toward self-defined health and want to get better.

FIGURE 1.

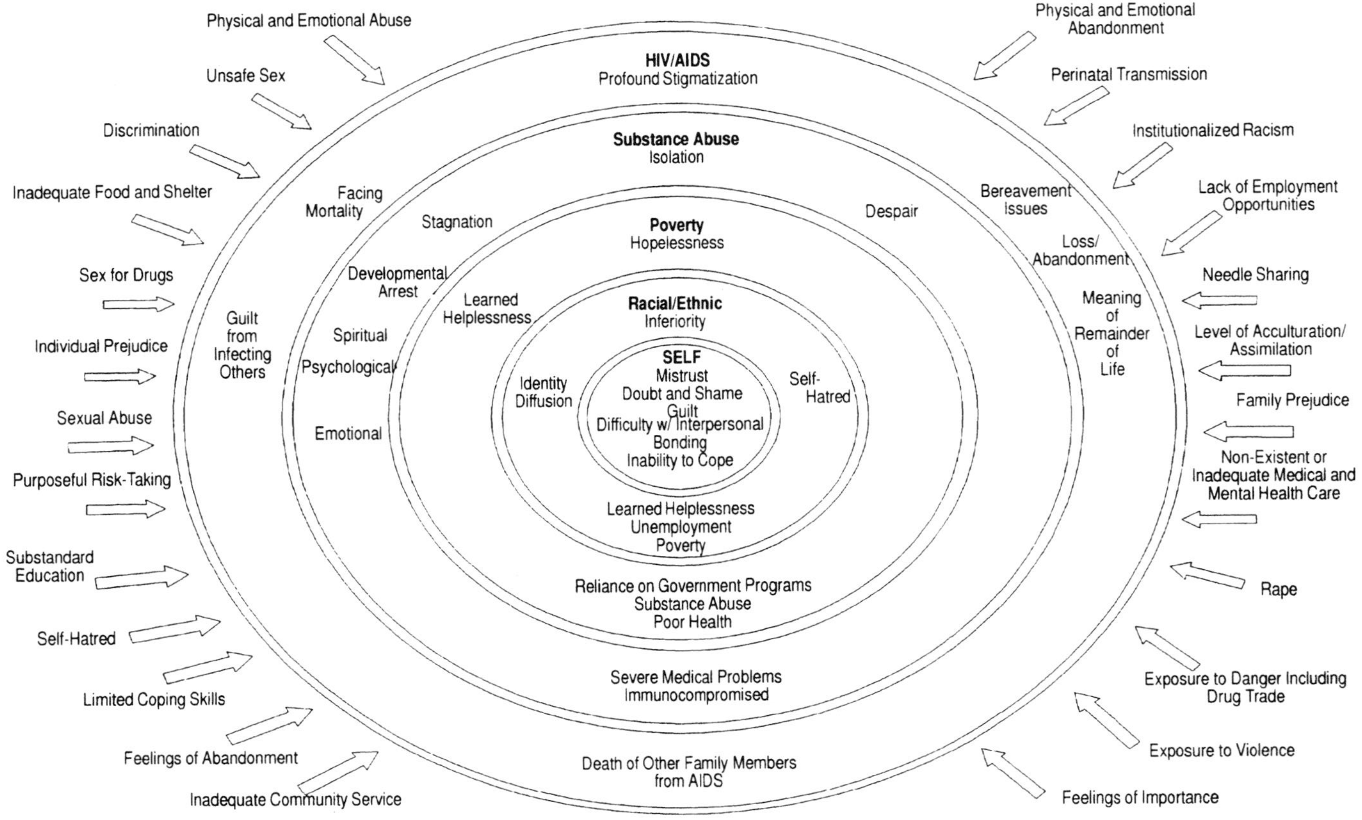

Physical and Emotional Abuse
Unsafe Sex
Discrimination
Inadequate Food and Shelter
Sex for Drugs
Individual Prejudice
Sexual Abuse
Purposeful Risk-Taking
Substandard Education
Self-Hatred
Limited Coping Skills
Feelings of Abandonment
Inadequate Community Service
Physical and Emotional Abandonment
Perinatal Transmission
Institutionalized Racism
Lack of Employment Opportunities
Needle Sharing
Level of Acculturation/ Assimilation
Family Prejudice
Non-Existent or Inadequate Medical and Mental Health Care
Rape
Exposure to Danger Including Drug Trade
Exposure to Violence
Feelings of Importance
HIV/AIDS
Profound Stigmatization
Guilt from Infecting Others
Facing Mortality
Bereavement Issues
Loss/ Abandonment
Meaning of Remainder of Life
Severe Medical Problems
Immunocompromised
Death of Other Family Members from AIDS
Substance Abuse
Isolation
Stagnation
Developmental Arrest
Spiritual
Psychological
Emotional
Despair
Reliance on Government Programs
Substance Abuse
Poor Health
Poverty
Hopelessness
Learned Helplessness
Racial/Ethnic
Inferiority
Identity Diffusion
Self- Hatred
Learned Helplessness
Unemployment
Poverty
SELF
Mistrust
Doubt and Shame
Guilt
Difficulty w/ Interpersonal Bonding
Inability to Cope

The authors' work has been influenced by the humanistic psychology of Abraham Maslow (1954; 1968), and Carl Rogers (1961), and by the interpersonal theory of Harry Stack Sullivan (1953). Erik Erikson's (1959) epigenetic conception of ego development, which emphasizes psychosocial influences, has been directly applied to our treatment model.

LAYOUT

The MMO presents a total of seven layers of oppression: four are "Individual Context" factors while three are "Outcome" factors.

The "Individual Context" factors (the self, gender, race/ethnicity, sexual orientation) are related to the identity of the individual, are more stable over time, and are influenced by genetics and upbringing. The "Outcome" factors (poverty, substance abuse, and HIV/AIDS) are results of social, behavioral and institutional influences that result from memberships in these oppressed groups.

These factors are all considered "layers of oppressed group membership." Concentric circles are used to illustrate the layers' cumulative effect on the person. Each circle or layer depicts three major domains of analysis relevant to that respective oppressed group membership. These are (see Figure 2):

1. Environmental influences–Pressures from various expectations in the person's environment (e.g., family, friends, society).
2. Intrapsychic processes–The persons' feelings, thoughts, emotional and cognitive reactions.
3. Behavioral/clinical manifestations–The person's behavior in reaction to the environmental influences and intrapsychic processes.

We find the visual display of this material helpful for two reasons. First, it attempts to consolidate an abundance of relevant and overlapping clinical material into a rational order. Second, the clinician can observe at a glance the complex array of immediate problems facing the client simultaneously. The layers of oppression are conceived as dynamic, since the focus of the work will shift as different layers take the forefront in the life, and subsequently the

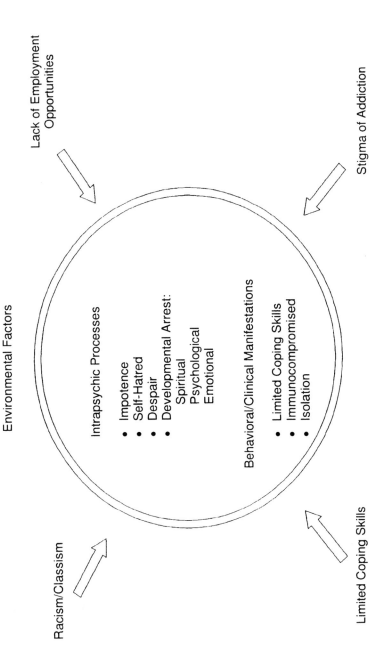

FIGURE 2. Substance Abuse (Outcome)

Environmental Factors

Lack of Employment Opportunities

Stigma of Addiction

Racism/Classism

Limited Coping Skills

Intrapsychic Processes

- Impotence
- Self-Hatred
- Despair
- Developmental Arrest:
  Spiritual
  Psychological
  Emotional

Behavioral/Clinical Manifestations

- Limited Coping Skills
- Immunocompromised
- Isolation

treatment, of the MOPWA. It is critical to recognize the patients' internalization of the negative views about the different layers, as this will interfere with their ability to work through the treatment process.

LAYERS OF OPPRESSION

Individual Context

The Individual Context layers are interrelated parts of the person's identity. They are integral to the definition of the person and are relatively intractable.

1. Self–This layer addresses the development of the individual's sense of worth and of self. It also involves the development of coping skills and ego defenses. Developmental theorists such as Erikson (1959) discussed the impact of the early caretaker relationships on the person's understanding and feelings about self in dealing with the world. The way in which basic needs were met or not met as a child strongly influences the individual's self concept and determines whether the world is seen as safe or hostile.

Many of the patients described here have been reared by caretakers who have been non-nurturing because they remain in their own struggle with the various issues of multiple oppressed group memberships. Knowledge of the historical-familial repetition of the inability to negotiate these memberships is critical because it provides a window into the coping styles that are modeled for the patients throughout their lives, while also making sense of current family dynamics. For example, Juan's family members know that he needs all of his monthly SSI check to pay for basic life necessities like food and shelter. Despite this, they routinely contact him for drug money on the day he receives the check. Juan feels overwhelmed and helpless when his family does this and he believes that he needs to acquiesce to their unreasonable and abusive demands or risk losing them completely. "Familisimo" dictates that the welfare of the family is placed before that of the individual (Zayas & Palleja, 1988), making it especially difficult for Juan to set limits on even unreasonable demands without experiencing profound guilt. This demonstrates a cultural expectation that is exacerbated by the dysfunction of his particular family. In treatment, Juan's understanding of this dichotomy and of his own victimization, have improved his self-esteem by enabling him to see that he is not to blame for their behavior. When asked for money now, Juan explains that he has personal expenses to attend to. When he recently moved, he chose not to give family members his address or phone number. These are ways that Juan feels he can better control the nature of the contact he has with his family. Juan has started to understand that they will probably not change and as treatment progresses he will be encouraged to maintain a separateness that provides him with valuable family contact, while minimizing the opportunities for abuse. Juan is also engaged in an ongoing grief process focused on feelings connected to his family's inability to nurture him.

As children, patients were often left alone or brought up by other family members. Many did not receive adequate food on a regular basis and at times even shelter was uncertain. Most patients have developed coping styles consistent with early childhood trauma due to physical and emotional abuse (including sexual abuse), neglect and abandonment (often by chemically dependent caretakers) and routine exposure to violence. These coping styles include but are not limited to, denial, rationalization, intellectualization, and minimization. The use of these primitive defenses into adulthood may be skillful and necessary ways of surviving in a very threatening and hostile environment, though interpersonal bonding is clearly affected. Erikson (1959) described some of the negative outcomes of early age difficulties with the world as mistrust, doubt and shame and guilt. All future relationships will be negotiated within this framework. In psychotherapy, the therapist is symbolic of "parent." Patients express concern about whether the therapist will really "be there" for them or if the pattern of other relationships they have had will be repeated and they will be abandoned.

As cited earlier, Juan's history of abuse and the many losses and betrayals he has experienced define the way he makes relationships. From the start, Juan wanted to be a "good" patient, announcing that he wouldn't burden the therapist with some of the horrible experiences he had as a child. He wanted to take care of the therapist (a powerful authority figure) by telling her what he thought she wanted to hear. Most of all he didn't want to cause her any trouble or have her get angry by being too demanding. Juan thought that this type of behavior (or even negative thoughts), would cause the therapist to determine him unworthy of treatment and she would abandon him. He also appeared terrified of exposing his rage which has become buried under "nice" behaviors towards authority figures. Group treatment has focused on creating a safe emotional climate in the sessions, where the therapist openly acknowledges Juan's fears of driving her away, while also encouraging him to take risks by getting closer. Missed sessions are viewed not only as resistance to treatment, but as self care, following difficult sessions, usually when Juan's negative sense of himself is explored or when reality testing challenges the nature of his family's contact with him.

2. Gender–The social and cultural role expectations of members of both genders and the prevalence of gender based societal discrimination have an impact on the patient. Women in America still do not have opportunities equal to men and this situation for women of color is further compounded by racism, which constitutes a double oppression. Awareness of cultural definitions of gender roles are important in understanding the dynamics of women of color. The struggle to confront current life situations frequently forces these women to negotiate traditional roles and behaviors in the interest of the advancement of their family.

Women in general are viewed as caretakers. In the African American family, this involves caring for the extended family, which includes non-blood relatives such as friends, godparents, or neighbors (Boyd-Franklin, 1989). Some of Cherie's "siblings" were her maternal cousins whom her mother felt obligated to take in when Cherie's aunt died. As one of the older girls in the family, Cherie helped raise her younger siblings, even visiting them in jail when her parents refused to. Cherie has extended her role as caretaker to current relationships. She offers her apartment to acquaintances who have become temporarily homeless, she lends money to friends in need, and she cares for her husband who is in end stage AIDS. In many of these instances she is not thanked and at times has been "taken" by well meaning "friends." Her judgement is skewed by her almost insatiable need to help others. Cherie seems to be driven by her sense of responsibility, stemming from her role as one of the heroes in her alcoholic family of origin. When she is betrayed, she becomes overwhelmed and anxious, sometimes using dangerous street drugs to cope. Treatment has included stabilizing Cherie's random drug use in order for group psychotherapy to proceed. A staff psychiatrist substituted prescription medication, while weaning her off illegal drugs. Through group therapy, Cherie has been encouraged to explore her own needs which she minimizes or denies. She is working towards asking for support in appropriate ways from healthy, available people, in an effort to find a better balance between nurturing others and allowing them to nurture her. As a mother herself, Cherie has not raised her own children. They remain in kinship foster care with an aunt, an apparent reversal of her own mother's position. In placing her children (due to substance abuse), Cherie may be acting out her resentment at her family for having had to raise their children before even having her own.

3. Race/Ethnicity–The patients described in this paper are mostly Black and Latino. It is critical to explore the patients' feelings about their race and ethnicity. Various theories of racial (Helms, 1983; Parham, 1989) and ethnic (Atkinson, Morton and Sue, 1989) identity development have been posited to describe the need for a person to come to terms with their racial/ethnic identity, in order to establish an integrated and positive sense of self.

Many of the patients have negative feelings about their racial/ethnic group membership. America has historically discriminated against people of color and racism has become institutionalized in this country. The white majority culture consistently communicates to people of color that who they are is not good enough, suggesting that they become someone whom they are not, and whom they can never be. The patient is put in a double bind and their sense of competence and identity is affected.

The internalization of eurocentrism has made skin color and hair texture an issue for both Blacks and Latinos. Lighter skin and straighter hair is associated with being closer to the white ideal and ultimately to being more worthy or valuable. Some very light skinned Latinos and African-Americans may make an effort to "pass" as white persons. Cherie told her white therapist as soon as she met her that her best helpers have been white. She referred to the therapists' hair as "good hair" because it is straight.

The therapist working with patients of color in group treatment must be available to process this highly charged material with the patient. This requires the therapist to honestly examine his or her own racism, a difficult process which is generally not understood by mental health professionals, because it has often not been a part of their routine training. Supervisors (even those of color) often remain unaware of the dynamics of such a process, and many therapists are taught to essentially treat patients in a "color blind" manner. At best, cultural differences among patients are noticed. But racism must really be understood as having a profound impact on the relationship between patient and therapist, since it helps to define the power differential in the therapeutic relationship. Cherie has been encouraged to explore the references she makes to racial themes. She has been able to do so only minimally, but as trust builds the therapist is hopeful that more can be examined. Cherie is faced with a dichotomy of feelings. While she fears that the therapist will terminate her treatment if her underlying rage leaks out, she is simultaneously struggling with her own rageful thoughts against the therapist whom she needs but may feel like annihilating. Group therapy offers Cherie the opportunity to align herself with other patients who may acknowledge the effects of racism in their treatment, either in the large system or in individual or group therapy. Also the group may offer Cherie the support she needs to take risks in revealing her feelings. Underlying self hatred, fueled by a society that values whites more, impedes the process of honest communication, as does countertransference which can keep the therapist from exploring group feelings, since it may evoke the feeling of being "ganged up on." The unaware therapist may in fact sabotage any discussion about race, feeling too threatened to look at his or her own racism and or rage.

Family prejudice, stemming from the patient's caretakers' own internalization of oppression and self hatred (Jorge, 1985; Millan, 1994), is another factor in shaping the negative (racial/ethnic) self image. Understanding the patient's perception of their ethnic identity will also provide information regarding level of assimilation. Issues such as language dominance, and adherence to cultural traditions and values are of importance here. Newly arrived immigrants use the context of their home country as the reference point for the rules of interaction. They may not be aware of the social norms, cues and rituals which help facilitate negotiation of systems. On the other hand, assimilated persons have taken on American values and norms completely, leaving their own cultural traditions, norms and values behind. In some families, Spanish-speaking parents insist that their children speak only English in an effort to maximize their ability to "make it" in America. The underlying message that is communicated to the child is that they are not good enough unless they speak English. Bicultural persons negotiate two cultures and take on the best points of each, including the language of both. Many of the patients describe experiences of switching back and forth between roles and behaviors in order to negotiate particular situations.

4. Sexual Orientation—Various developmental theories describing the process of integrating a gay/lesbian identity (e.g., Morales, 1992; Coleman, 1983) are useful in comprehending the issues faced by the gay or lesbian patient. Previously discussed gender and cultural expectations impact on the person's understanding and negotiation of a gay or lesbian identity, as does the internalization of heterosexism.

Morales (1992) spoke of Latino gays and Latina lesbians as living within three communities: the gay and lesbian community, the Latino community and the predominantly White heterosexual mainstream society.

Many Latino and Black men who have sex with men describe feeling discriminated against at gay organizations which are predominantly White. They report frustration and anger about this reaction to their race and/or ethnicity by people they feel should be more supportive. Also, within Black and Latino communities, there is a bias against homosexuality, generating further feelings of isolation. These feelings are brought into group psychotherapy, as the patient may view the therapist as also holding the heterosexist views of the society and family (Maylon, 1983). This creates negative transference that must be worked through. It also requires therapists to own their homophobic/heterosexist feelings so they do not interfere countertransferentially.

Historically, Juan has been unable to understand or express his sexuality in a clear way. His father called him derogatory names as a child and ridiculed his effeminate manner. Juan wonders about the effect the kidnapping (which included extensive sexual abuse by a man) has had on his sexual orientation. As a teenager, Juan had sex with both male and female partners. He describes the encounters with girls as attempts to satisfy his family's expectations of him, and he was aware that he was mostly attracted to boys during this time. Juan spent his middle twenties in jail, where he had sex with men (this is how he contracted HIV). He feels that he knew that he was homosexual then but he didn't "come out" because it was not safe, and because he didn't need to. Sex was available in jail anyway. After jail he moved away from his family, and he dressed in drag. He described himself as being a "flame" then, but says that he felt happy and sometimes misses that life.

Latino families generally do not talk with their children about sex (Millán and Rabiner, 1992). Since homosexuality is a subject that is even more taboo, gay Latino men have few opportunities to dialogue openly about their sexual orientation with peers and family members whom they do not want to embarrass by their "coming out." So when Juan decided to tell his family that he was gay, he expected a strong reaction from them. Instead, he says that "they are cool about it," and that they don't talk much about it, and haven't mentioned it to him again. The message appeared to be that the only way they could deal with the news was to veil it in secrecy in hopes that it would go away. Juan no longer dresses in drag, and he says he would like everyone else to assume he is straight. Juan has not had a lover in several years, explaining that he does not want to infect anyone with HIV. His internalized homophobia may have resonated with his family's reaction and he too chose to downplay his gay identity.

In the early stages of treatment, Juan alluded to being gay, though he didn't talk openly about it. He needed to assess the therapist's comfort with this and probably feared being rejected by the therapist. He even brought lunch for the two to share during the session. He could not explore the reasons for his behavior at that point in the treatment other than to say he just wanted to bring the therapist lunch. He may have needed to relate in a manner which he felt was more traditionally "male" so that the therapist would accept him. Juan eventually stated he was gay, in almost a whisper, and continued that he didn't want other people to know about it. He told the therapist he was afraid of being ostracized within his community and of being the victim of gay bashing on the street. Juan probably also had a concern that this would also occur in the treatment.

Therapy will focus on the area of self acceptance, always with an understanding of the cultural issues involved. The core issue of sexual identity is one in which the patient must be given the opportunity to explore both positive and negative feelings about their sexual orientation (Maylon, 1983). It is important that the therapist remain open to the myriad of complex issues that converge to form a person's sexual identity which is a major component of their psychological makeup.

OUTCOME VARIABLES

1. Poverty–The socioeconomic variable of poverty puts our patients in the lowest class, and society automatically makes a judgement about their unworthiness. Class is a very salient factor in a person's ability to move through American society and achieve success. Inadequate food and shelter is consistent with poverty and it affects the physical and mental well being of many patients. Medical problems may result from an inadequate diet and inadequate housing. In the neighborhoods where our patients live, the schools are typically overcrowded, understaffed and lack even basic supplies like paper, pencils and books. The dropout rate is high and many high school graduates find few if any employment opportunities. Within this level of oppression there is a solidification of the self hatred and the feelings of inferiority, which creates a sense of profound despair and exacerbates risk-taking behavior.

Cherie comes from a working class family where she completed high school and worked "off and on" until around the age of 25 when she became drug addicted. Her addiction created the disorganization which led her to lose her job and go on welfare. Cherie often expresses her anger at people who judge those on welfare. It is clear that she is also angry at herself for becoming drug addicted. Her lower class status has demoted her to a place of even more powerlessness. Her life revolves around large systems that do not respect her: substance abuse treatment, public assistance, and the child welfare agency. Cherie maintains contact with her children but she rarely talks about them in the group. She appears to be guilty and embarrassed about having given them up. Guilt and issues of loss are the main themes in group therapy with Cherie. These are the very same themes from her childhood and they are further exacerbated by her husband's AIDS condition and her own HIV status.

2. Substance Abuse–Many of the patients related feeling that the "drug addict" label is the most stigmatizing for them. They describe frequent encounters in which they feel judged and discriminated against because of their drug abuse history. These feelings must be explored because they may also be defensive in nature, employed to avoid confronting a challenge or obstacle. They may also be the internalization of society's negative view of substance abusers. Much of the work in group therapy is to help the patients feel good enough about themselves so that they will attempt more constructive behaviors.

Many patients describe the onset of their drug use as an effort to self-medicate painful feelings. The drugs function as a coping mechanism, or a defense, which temporarily empowers them. Through the action of obtaining and using the drug, patients are able to take care of themselves. Artificial bonds are formed with fellow users and an illusion of safety and intimacy may be achieved. Although drug use may provide short-term relief, the long-term consequences of addiction are both debilitating and stigmatizing for the multiply oppressed patient. Unlike those in the upper classes of society, there are fewer safety nets (supportive families, employment and treatment opportunities) to hold the effects of addiction at bay. Addiction also inhibits the development of healthier coping mechanisms which encourage choice and self-direction. Since feelings are numbed, spiritual, psychological and emotional arrest occur, leaving the person unable to sufficiently establish a meaningful relationship with themselves or others, and without a viable and self-respecting way to manage the world. For the addicted MOPWA, any hope for a constructive sober future is now complicated by the oppression of being terminally ill. Also, the drugs of choice for the

MOPWA tend to cause a serious decline in overall health in a short period of time.

In Cherie's case, there was a family history of addiction, with both of her parents being alcoholic. She experimented with alcohol herself and was introduced to heroin at age 17 by some older siblings and cousins. Cherie's recollections of her involvement with drugs, which she has discussed in group, demonstrate the perceived positive experiences associated with drugs, including adventure and friendship, especially during the recreational phase of her use. Admittedly, she began to have problems with drugs when she became addicted and lost control. She began to use pills in her mid-twenties and entered methadone treatment after losing her children. A medical problem forced her to stop drinking completely. She was in pain and in danger of dying. While she continues to struggle with the intermittent use of pills, a harm reduction approach (Springer, 1991) has been employed in group therapy and has resulted in very infrequent lapses. Cherie remains stressed, but now she uses both the interpersonal relationships she has developed in the group and her own renewed self-confidence (a by-product of recovery), as ways of coping. She talks more openly about her pain and she acknowledges her accomplishments, most notably, her personal growth.

Juan was introduced to drugs by the man who kidnapped him when he was a boy. By the time he escaped he had a heroin habit. He later used alcohol and cocaine sporadically. Juan began methadone treatment after leaving jail, during which time he discovered he was HIV+. He has been free of all secondary substances since entering methadone treatment and he believes that any drug use will lower his T-cells. One fascinating aspect of Juan's abstinence is his ability to manage feelings of post-traumatic stress disorder without using illegal drugs. Juan is prescribed medication for sleep, which he finds effective. His early associations with drugs were negative. As a child he saw his father drink and get violent. Drugs were forced on him when he was held captive. He used other drugs briefly "by choice" but he never really lived a "drug lifestyle." Juan is currently able to manage very painful feelings related to his traumatic past, without using illegal drugs. His abstinence may signify an inner strength or resiliency that motivates him to seek functional interpersonal relationships with both natural and professional helpers, as a way of coping.

As these two examples indicate, each patient's way of using drugs is fashioned by the nuances of their own psychosocial history. Contrary to popular belief, all addicts are not the same! The patient must be encouraged to articulate the meaning drugs have had in their life. For Cherie drugs were both an effective way to manage feelings and a way to have fun, until they turned on her, as they inevitably do. Juan did not choose to use drugs and initially they took the role of yet another perpetrator. We believe a generic, one-size-fits-all, substance abuse treatment protocol is doomed to fail because it doesn't sufficiently analyze an individual's underlying motivations for using drugs in the first place. The MMO is one attempt to look at substance abuse within the context of the whole person.

3. HIV/AIDS–The patient becomes infected with the HIV virus through various risk factors which are noted on the outside of the circle. The risk taking behavior is connected to all that has been discussed thus far, including low self-esteem, involvement in the drug culture and a sense of hopelessness and despair. Patients often feel like they deserve to be infected with HIV and becoming HIV-positive may, for some, be a self-fulfilling prophecy. Being HIV-positive may trigger a life review originally thought to occur at old age (Erikson, 1959). The task for the patient is to negotiate "their one and only life cycle and how it turned out." The HIV-infected person begins to deal with their own mortality the instant that they receive their test results, though many never engage in this process consciously throughout the entire course of the illness. For the MOPWA, this can be simply because they are too busy with survival issues to engage in the process or because they generally feel a significant amount of shame and guilt about their life. In psychotherapy, the patient is encouraged to make a conscious effort to engage in the life review process. The group therapist must assess each patient's ego strength to determine the extent of the life review.

The MOPWA typically experiences massive bereavement, because so many of their loved ones are also HIV-infected. Cherie's case is a good example. Several siblings and friends are infected, some have died, and her husband is currently in the end stages of the illness. Much of treatment constitutes ongoing grief work and the therapist must have a good working knowledge of the psychological effects of massive bereavement, which include psychic numbing, feelings of hopelessness and despair, and symptoms of PTSD. The integration of fresh loss into the grieving process that is already underway is not sufficiently understood (Rando, 1986; Worden, 1982). The process that Cherie is going through has no clear predecessor. There are similarities to veterans of combat in military conflicts, and to families dealing with terminal illness in general, but the stigmatizing and pervasive nature of HIV in her family makes the treatment process difficult and unclear. Cherie has been encouraged by the group to talk about the losses and to share her painful feelings. When one of the therapists recently terminated with the group, Cherie was unable to attend those sessions to say goodbye. Upon her return, though, she was able to admit the difficulty of ending this important relationship. For the MOPWA, loss is an everpresent reality and a raw nerve.

Therapists also have to address countertransferential feelings about extensive work with death and dying issues. Many providers describe feeling "burned out" unless they have established support systems for themselves through supervision, therapy, and other interests.

CONCLUSION

MOPWA's present a myriad of issues which must be simultaneously negotiated including their struggle with the internalization of the negative views that their oppressed group memberships have exposed them to. As the two case studies have demonstrated, the various layers of oppressed group memberships constitute a formidable challenge for the therapist throughout the group treatment process.

REFERENCES

Atkinson, D.R., Morton, G. and Sue, D.W. (1989). *Counseling minorities: A cross cultural perspective.* Third Ed. Dubuque, IA: Wm. C. Brown Publishers.
Boyd-Franklin, N. (1989). *Black families in therapy: A multisystems approach.* New York: Guilford Press.

Centers for Disease Control and Prevention (1995, April). *HIV/AIDS surveillance report.*

Coleman, E. (1983). Developmental stages of the coming out process. In J.C. Gonsiorek (Ed.), *A guide to psychotherapy with gay and lesbian clients* (pp. 31-43). NY: Harrington Park Press.

Elia, N. & Millán, F. (1995, June). *Group therapy with HIV infected methadone patients.* Paper presented at the 2nd International AIDS Impact Conference, Brighton, England.

Erikson, E.H. (1959). *Identity and the lifecycle.* New York: W. W. Norton.

Helms, J.E. (1984). Toward a theoretical explanation of the effects of race on counseling: A Black and White model. *Psychological Bulletin, 83* (2), 338-352.

Jorge, A. (1985). The Black Puerto Rican woman in contemporary American society. New York: Praeger.

Kastenbaum, R.J. (1977). Death and development through the life span. In H. Feigel (Ed.), *New meanings of life* (pp. 35-47). New York: McGraw-Hill.

Lehman, V., & Russell, N. (1985). Psychological and social issues of AIDS. In V. Gong (Ed.), *Understanding AIDS* (pp. 177-182). New Brunswick, NJ: Rutgers University Press.

Maslow, A. H. (1954). *Motivation and personality.* New York: Harper.

Maslow, A. H. (1968). *Towards a psychology of being.* (2nd. ed.) Princeton: Van Nostrand.

Maylon, A.K. (1983). Psychotherapeutic implications of internalized homophobia in gay men. In J.C. Gosnorek (Ed.), *A guide to psychotherapy with gay and lesbian clients.* NY: Harrington Park Press.

Millán, F. (1995, April). *Mental health implications of racism for Latinos.* Paper presented at the 71st Annual Meeting of the American Orthopsychiatric Association Meeting, Washington, D.C.

Millán, F. & Elia, N. (1994). *The model of multiple oppression: Theoretical framework.* Unpublished manuscript.

Millán, F. & Spence Rabiner, S. (1992). Toward a culturally sensitive child sexual abuse prevention program for Latinos. *Journal of Social Distress and the Homeless,* 1 (3/4).

Morales, E. S. (1992). Counseling Latino gays and Latina lesbians. In S.H. Dworkin & F.J. Gutierrez (Eds.) *Counseling gay men and lesbians: Journey to the end of the rainbow.* (pp. 125-139). Alexandria, VA: American Counseling Association.

New York State Department of Health (1995, March). *AIDS surveillance quarterly update.* NY: Bureau of HIV/AIDS Epidemiology of the NYS Department of Health.

Parham, J.A. (1989). Cycles of psychological nigrescence. *The Counseling Psychologist,* 17 (2) 187-226.

Rando, T. A. (1986). *Loss and Anticipatory Grief.* Lexington, Mass: Lexington Books.

Rogers, C.R. (1961). *On becoming a person.* Boston: Houghton Mifflin.

Springer, E. (1991). Counseling chemically dependent people with HIV illness. *Journal of Chemical Dependency Treatment, 4*(2).

Sullivan, H.S. (1953). *The interpersonal theory of psychiatry.* New York: Norton.

Volkan, V.D., & Zintl, E. (1993). *Life after loss: the lessons of grief.* Scribner, Macmillan.

Worden, J. W. (1982). *Grief Counseling and Grief Therapy.* New York: Springer Publishers.

Zayas, L. H. & Palleja, J. (1988). Puerto Rican familism: Considerations for family therapy. *Family Relations, 37*(3), 260-264.

Index

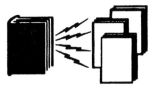

Haworth
DOCUMENT DELIVERY
SERVICE

This valuable service provides a single-article order form for any article from a Haworth journal.

- *Time Saving:* No running around from library to library to find a specific article.
- *Cost Effective:* All costs are kept down to a minimum.
- *Fast Delivery:* Choose from several options, including same-day FAX.
- *No Copyright Hassles:* You will be supplied by the original publisher.
- *Easy Payment:* Choose from several easy payment methods.

Open Accounts Welcome for . . .
- Library Interlibrary Loan Departments
- Library Network/Consortia Wishing to Provide Single-Article Services
- Indexing/Abstracting Services with Single Article Provision Services
- Document Provision Brokers and Freelance Information Service Providers

---

MAIL or *FAX* THIS ENTIRE ORDER FORM TO:

Haworth Document Delivery Service
The Haworth Press, Inc.
10 Alice Street
Binghamton, NY 13904-1580

or FAX: 1-800-895-0582
or CALL: 1-800-342-9678
9am-5pm EST

PLEASE SEND ME PHOTOCOPIES OF THE FOLLOWING SINGLE ARTICLES:

1) Journal Title: _____
   Vol/Issue/Year: _____Starting & Ending Pages:_____
   Article Title:_____

2) Journal Title: _____
   Vol/Issue/Year: _____Starting & Ending Pages:_____
   Article Title:_____

3) Journal Title: _____
   Vol/Issue/Year: _____Starting & Ending Pages:_____
   Article Title:_____

4) Journal Title: _____
   Vol/Issue/Year: _____Starting & Ending Pages:_____
   Article Title:_____

(See other side for Costs and Payment Information)

COSTS: Please figure your cost to order quality copies of an article.

1. Set-up charge per article: $8.00
    ($8.00 × number of separate articles)   _____

2. Photocopying charge for each article:

    1-10 pages: $1.00   _____

    11-19 pages: $3.00   _____

    20-29 pages: $5.00   _____

    30+ pages: $2.00/10 pages   _____

3. Flexicover (optional): $2.00/article   _____

4. Postage & Handling: US: $1.00 for the first article/
                        $.50 each additional article   _____

    Federal Express: $25.00   _____

    Outside US: $2.00 for first article/
    $.50 each additional article   _____

5. Same-day FAX service: $.35 per page   _____

                        GRAND TOTAL: _____

METHOD OF PAYMENT: (please check one)

❑ Check enclosed   ❑ Please ship and bill. PO # _____
                   (sorry we can ship and bill to bookstores only! All others must pre-pay)

❑ Charge to my credit card: ❑ Visa; ❑ MasterCard; ❑ Discover;
                             ❑ American Express;

Account Number:_____ Expiration date:_____

Signature: ✗_____

Name: _____ Institution: _____

Address: _____

_____

City: _____ State:_____ Zip:_____

Phone Number: _____ FAX Number: _____

MAIL or *FAX* THIS ENTIRE ORDER FORM TO:

Haworth Document Delivery Service	**or FAX:** 1-800-895-0582
The Haworth Press, Inc.	**or CALL:** 1-800-342-9678
10 Alice Street	9am-5pm EST)
Binghamton, NY 13904-1580	